Super Bowl Superstars

The Most Valuable Players in the NFL's Championship Game

Super Bowl Superstars

The Most Valuable Players in the NFL's Championship Game

by Pete Alfano

illustrated with photographs

A Zander Hollander Sports Book

RANDOM HOUSE   NEW YORK

Library of Congress Cataloging in Publication Data:
Alfano, Pete. Super Bowl superstars
(The Random House sports library) "A Zander Hollander sports book."
  SUMMARY: A brief history of the Super Bowl highlighting the contributions of fifteen stars voted Most Valuable Players in these championship games. 1. Super Bowl Game (Football)—Juvenile literature. 2. Football players—United States—Biography—Juvenile literature. [1. Super Bowl Game (Football) 2. Football players]
I. Title. II. Series. GV956.2.S8A43 796.332'78 82-368
ISBN: 0-394-85017-3 (pbk.); 0-394-95017-8 (lib. bdg.) AACR2

Manufactured in the United States of America   1   2   3   4   5   6   7   8   9   0

Contents

Introduction

It is not just another Sunday in January; it is called Super Sunday. On that day the Super Bowl is held—the single most popular sports event in America. It does not matter whether a person lives in Green Bay, Wisconsin, New York City, or in a place that does not have a professional football team; all activity stops on Super Sunday.

City streets are unusually quiet and country roads are empty while the Super Bowl is played. Football fans as well as those who cannot tell the difference between a football and a basketball sit in front of their television sets, munching on goodies and watching the action.

What is so amazing is that the people who run professional football did not expect the Super Bowl to become so big. The game was arranged in 1966, when the established National Football League (NFL) agreed to merge with the younger American Football League (AFL). The champions of both leagues would meet in a title game to be played in January.

But the owners in both leagues could not decide on a name for this special game. They wanted an exciting name, something that would describe how important a game it would be. A little girl helped them find the answer.

She was the daughter of Lamar Hunt, owner of the AFL's Kansas City Chiefs. One night Hunt brought home a gift for his daughter, a Silly Putty ball that bounced crazily. "It's my super ball, Dad," the little girl told her father. That gave Hunt an idea.

At the next owners' meeting he said, "Why not call it the Super Bowl?" Everyone agreed.

Now, every January, fans all around the country look forward to the Super Bowl. The stadium where it is played is usually in a warm climate where there is little chance of snow or rain.

This is the story of the Most Valuable Players (MVP's) of the Super Bowl. In every Super Bowl the sportswriters select an MVP, the player they feel has done the most to help his team. These are the superstars who make the Super Bowl worth watching and Super Sunday one of the most action-packed days of the year.

Super Bowl Superstars

The Most Valuable Players in the NFL's Championship Game

Bart Starr
A Starr Is Born

He was the son of an Air Force sergeant, a quiet, disciplined youngster who showed at an early age that he intended to live up to his name. Bart Starr was a high-school All-America quarterback in Montgomery, Alabama, and shone as a freshman and sophomore at the University of Alabama. But injuries plagued him, and by the time he was a senior he had become a bench-warmer, replaced by a younger quarterback.

The professional teams were so unimpressed with him that Bart was not chosen until the seventeenth round of the 1956 draft, when the Green Bay Packers decided to take a chance on him.

Although the Packers were NFL doormats in those days, they gave Starr little opportunity to play. They preferred to use veteran quarterbacks. But in 1959 the Packers hired a coach, Vince Lombardi, who not only gave Starr new life but made the Packers the most glamorous team of the 1960s.

With Starr as the quarterback, the Packers won NFL titles in 1961, 1962, 1965, and 1966. Now they were headed for Los Angeles to take on the Kansas City Chiefs of the American Football League in the first Super Bowl.

It had been two weeks since the Packers and the Chiefs had won their league championships, and the teams were getting impatient to play in Super Bowl I. It seemed that the day would never come. Even a veteran quarterback like Bart Starr, a patient man, was beginning to get edgy.

This was developing into more than just a football game anyway. A circus atmosphere surrounded both teams the week before the game. Hundreds of newspaper reporters and television crews were on hand to record the players' every word or grunt or groan. There were Super Bowl parties every night as the countdown went on.

Before leaving Kansas City, the Chiefs had been victims of burglars who broke into their offices and stole money from a safe. They hoped that would be their only loss.

The Packers were an experienced team, used to performing in big games. But even they could not be prepared for what greeted them as they ran onto the playing field in the Los Angeles Coliseum on January 15, 1967. There was a giant marching band of more than 300 musicians. There were 80 baton twirlers. There were floats and glee clubs and photographers all around.

Above the field 400 pigeons, posing as doves, fluttered aimlessly before flying off in all directions, occasionally colliding with one another. They were meant to be symbols of peace between the leagues, but at this moment the birds were acting as if they had gone to all those Super Bowl parties.

Once the birds had flown away, however, the festivities ended and the game began. The Packers won the coin toss and, as usual, they chose to receive. "Coach Lombardi wants us to shove the ball down their throats before they shove it down ours," Packers' captain Bob Skoronski said.

But the Chiefs had a different idea. Starr was tackled twice on Green Bay's first series as the Packers failed to move the ball. He was not concerned, however. He knew the Chiefs had a weak defensive backfield and, with a little time, he could take advantage of it.

The opportunity came the very next time the Packers had the ball. It was on their 20-yard line. On second down, with the Chiefs looking for a running play, Starr dropped back and threw to tight end Marv Fleming over the middle. The play gained 11 yards and a first down. "The Pack" was beginning to roll.

Now, even when the Chiefs put pressure on Starr, he was able to slip away and somehow find an open receiver. First it was running back Elijah Pitts for 22 yards, then wide receiver Carroll Dale for 12 more. The Kansas City defense had been stopping the Packers' running attack, but Starr frustrated it with his expert passing. With a first down on the Chiefs' 37-yard line, he came up with another surprise. In the huddle, he called a passing play directed to Max McGee, a veteran who had played very little during the season.

McGee was in the game because Boyd Dowler had been injured. McGee was 34 and supposedly a broken-down player who could barely run. The night before the game he had sat in the hotel with his roommate, Paul Hornung, and wondered whether he was healthy enough to play an entire game.

"I don't know about my legs, Paul," he said. "I don't know if they'll hold up. But if Dowler gets hurt, I guess I'm the one who'll play."

The young defensive backs on the Chiefs were not paying much attention to McGee. So when the ball was snapped to Starr, Max made a couple of moves and got free. Starr threw a perfect pass that McGee caught and then carried 19 more yards to the end zone. The crowd cheered wildly, but the Packers took the touchdown in stride.

The Packers led, 7–0, and it looked as if all the experts were right: The young AFL champions were no match for this team.

Green Bay's Bart Starr threw two touchdown passes against Kansas City in Super Bowl I.

Len Dawson, though, was a veteran quarterback himself, one who was not going to lose his self-confidence under pressure. He rallied the Chiefs and answered the challenge. Kansas City's first good drive ended with a missed field-goal attempt, but early in the second quarter the Chiefs went on the march again. With a first down on the Packers' 38-yard line, Dawson completed a 31-yard pass to wide receiver Otis Taylor, who was tackled on the Green Bay seven-yard line.

The Chiefs were excited now, and they hurried out of the huddle for the next play. This time Dawson threw a touchdown pass to running back Curtis McClinton. The Chiefs celebrated as if they had won the game. On the sidelines Bart Starr and the rest of the Packer offense quietly discussed their next move.

Starr struck quickly. He stunned the Chiefs with a 64-yard touchdown pass to Carroll Dale. The touchdown was called back because of a penalty, but the damage had been done. The Kansas City defense crumbled as Starr moved the Packers to their second score. This time it was fullback Jim Taylor who ran 14 yards for the touchdown.

At halftime the Packers' lead was 14–10. The Chiefs had scored again when Mike Mercer kicked a 31-yard field goal.

During the intermission many of the 63,036 fans in the Coliseum talked about how unexpectedly close the game was. The Packers talked about it, too, in the locker room. They felt they were a much better team. They felt they were not proving it.

The Chiefs were gaining confidence. They took the second-half kickoff and began to move again. With a third down and five yards to go on their 49, Dawson dropped back and threw a pass to tight end Fred Arbanas. But Dawson did not see Willie Wood, the Packers' defensive back, who cut in front of Arbanas and intercepted the poorly thrown pass. Before the Chiefs could catch Wood, he had raced to their five-yard line.

This was Bart Starr's easiest drive so far. On first down he handed off to Pitts, who slashed his way through the defense for a touchdown. The Packers led, 21–10. The Chiefs now looked demoralized. Dawson was not getting enough protection, and the holes were closed for the running backs. The offense could not move.

Bart Starr sensed the change in mood. The game had swung the Packers' way. Now was the time to put it out of the Chiefs' reach. Starr did this in typical style. He picked apart the Chiefs little by little as if he were plucking the petals from a flower. He was not the daring passer that Johnny Unitas of the Colts was. Instead, he went about his business as if he were trying to put the Chiefs to sleep.

As the seconds ticked away in the third quarter, Starr mixed his passing and running plays to keep the defense off balance. The Chiefs needed the ball to get back into the game, and Starr would not let them have it. With less than a minute remaining in the quarter and the ball on the Kansas City 13-yard line, Starr passed to Max McGee for a touchdown. It was McGee's second touchdown in a game he never expected to play at all.

The score was 28–10, and the outcome no longer seemed in doubt. As the fourth quarter began, many fans headed for home convinced it would take a miracle for the Chiefs to catch up. Even several of the Kansas City players had given up.

"We should have gone home before it got messy," said Fred Williamson, the Chiefs' outspoken defensive back. "I knew it was hopeless."

Packer wide receiver Max McGee snags a Bart Starr pass in the end zone for his second touchdown.

Vince Lombardi did not take anything for granted, however. He kept Starr in the game, and the quarterback played as if the score was tied. He relied more on his running game to use up the clock, but he found his friend McGee in passing situations to keep a march going. Midway through the final quarter, Starr led the Packers on a 49-yard touchdown drive. Pitts scored from the one to give "The Pack" its final margin of victory. The score was 35–10.

Starr was voted the Most Valuable Player by the writers. He had completed 16 out of 23 passes for 250 yards and two touchdowns. "He was terrific," admitted Hank Stram, the losing coach. Starr was Lombardi's coach on the field, the one who put the plan into action. He'd made it possible for the Packers to win the first Super Bowl.

Bart Starr
The Perfect Finale

The cold had long since numbed his arms and legs. Even the heaters on the sidelines could not keep Bart Starr's hands warm. The temperature was 13 degrees below zero in Green Bay, Wisconsin, on December 31, 1967, as quarterback Starr's Packers battled the Dallas Cowboys for the NFL championship.

There was less than a minute left and the Cowboys led, 17–14, but Green Bay had a first down on the Dallas one-yard line. Two running plays failed to budge the Cowboys. Starr called a time-out. His team could attempt a field goal to tie the score and send the game into sudden-death overtime, but instead he and coach Vince Lombardi decided on the "thirty-one wedge," meaning Starr himself would carry the ball.

The Green Bay quarterback lowered his head and followed guard Jerry Kramer and tackle Forrest Gregg over the right side. He didn't look up until he landed in the end zone. The Packers had done it again. They were NFL *champions—by a 21–17 score—for the third year in a row. And on January 14, 1968, they would face the Oakland Raiders of the AFL in the Super Bowl.*

No one on the Packers was closer to Vince Lombardi than Bart Starr. It was Lombardi who'd given Starr a chance when most people believed that Starr was not an NFL quarterback. They were an odd couple: the fiery, loud Lombardi and the quiet, soft-spoken Starr. But they made a successful team.

The talk in Miami, Florida, before Super Bowl II was that Lombardi was going to retire after the game. Some of the great Packer stars like Paul Hornung had already retired, and others had just a year or two left. Starr himself was almost 34, and people were beginning to ask him how many more years he would play.

The Green Bay coach did not want to tell anyone what he would do but he also did not want all this talk of retirement to upset the players before such a big game. So in the locker room before the game, Lombardi gave the team a short speech. His voice was unusually low.

"I want to tell you how proud I am of all of you," he said. "It's been a long season, and this may be the last time we are all together." Some of the Packers had tears in their eyes.

It made them more determined to play their best against the Oakland Raiders. The AFL champions were considered a better team than the Kansas City Chiefs had been a year earlier. Oakland had lost only one game during the season. Owner Al Davis was a shrewd, wisecracking former coach who praised the Packers during Super Bowl Week but really expected his team to beat them.

Super Bowl II had its share of marching bands and baton twirlers. There were even a mechanical Green Bay Packer and Oakland Raider, each 30 feet high, that moved slowly across the Orange Bowl turf before the start of the game. White smoke came puffing out of their nostrils. The giants shook hands and then slowly puffed their way off the field.

The Packers respected the Raiders and expected a very physical game. Davis liked his team to throw its weight around. After their difficult season, however, and that last-second victory against the Cowboys, some of the Packers were not as motivated as usual.

"I just don't have the zip," tackle Forrest Gregg admitted. "It's been a long season. I feel like a robot."

But Green Bay was one of the most professional football teams, and Starr, despite his quiet manner, would not allow his teammates to give less than their best. The first time they had the ball, he moved them into field-goal range. Then Don Chandler, who had been acquired early in the 1965 season from the New York Giants, kicked a 39-yard field goal. Green Bay led, 3–0.

The defenses dominated play in the first quarter. Both teams moved the ball but neither could get close enough for a score. The Raiders were one of the highest-scoring teams in football, and quarterback Daryle Lamonica had an outstanding arm, yet the Packers kept frustrating them.

Near the end of the period, Starr began another of those long, methodical drives that were not very exciting to watch but were so effective. Throwing mostly to running back Donny Anderson and tight end Marv Fleming, he moved the Packers into scoring range. Those Raiders were stubborn, though. The Packers had to settle for another field goal by Chandler. Now their lead was 6–0.

On the sidelines Lombardi was becoming irritated. He wanted a touchdown. He did not think the Packers could win just by kicking field goals.

It was almost as if Starr had said, "Okay, Coach, one touchdown coming up." On a first-down play from his own 38-yard line, he faked a handoff into the line and then threw a long touchdown pass to Boyd Dowler. It took only 26 seconds for the Packers to score and raise their lead to 13–0.

The play looked so simple. None of the Raiders seemed to have been covering Dowler. "Kent McCloughan was," Dowler said. "He bumped me at the line of scrimmage and I just bulled past him. When I got by him, there was no one left to stop me."

The Raiders were an explosive team, however. They scored a touchdown on the next series when Lamonica passed 23 yards to wide receiver Bill Miller.

With 30 seconds left before halftime, the Packers received a break. Rodger Bird fumbled a punt and Green Bay recovered. Then Don Chandler kicked his third field goal, a 43-yarder, to give the Packers a 16–7 lead.

"I knew this would be my last game as a Packer," Chandler said later. "I was through as a player in my own mind. It was time to get to know my kids, build up my business, and plant some family roots."

Despite Chandler's contribution, Lombardi was angry at halftime. "Nine points!" he shouted. "That's not enough of a lead." He stormed into his office to meet with his assistant coaches.

Meanwhile, some of the older players, led by Starr, Dowler, Gregg, and Ray Nitschke, had their own private meeting. "Let's wrap this up for the old man," Starr said.

Now this veteran team was playing with emotion too. If

His receivers covered, Bart Starr scrambles for yardage against Oakland.

the Packers looked like robots, it was only because they rarely made a mistake. From their 18-yard line the Packers trudged down the field like pack mules, slowly, purposefully, eating up chunks of yardage like termites eat wood.

Starr was a surgeon, coolly dissecting the Oakland defense. But just when the Raiders thought he would never gamble, he did.

On third and one at the Green Bay 40, Starr faked a handoff and then threw a 35-yard pass to Max McGee. First down at the Oakland 25.

When the Packers returned to the huddle, Starr decided to call another passing play. "They don't know what to expect now," he said. "Let's throw again. They may be looking for the run."

He was right. He completed an 11-yard pass to Carroll Dale and a 12-yarder to Donny Anderson. On second down from the two, Anderson bolted into the end zone. The Packers were leading, 23–7. Before the third quarter ended, Chandler added his fourth field goal to make it 26–7.

More than 75,000 fans were watching a rout. Was the NFL this much better than the AFL? Or were the Packers just better than everyone?

The Green Bay defense, which had done an outstanding job of containing Lamonica, contributed some points of its own in the fourth quarter. Lamonica was desperate now, throwing long passes, needing touchdowns in a hurry. The Packers knew this and ignored Lamonica when he faked into the line. When the quarterback threw to Fred Biletnikoff, who was his favorite receiver, Herb Adderley stepped in and intercepted the pass. He stopped running 60 yards later when he reached the end zone. That made the score 33–7.

Bart Starr's day was over. He stood on the sidelines in the fourth quarter and watched like a fan. Victory was secure. Lamonica led the Raiders to one last touchdown, on a 23-yard pass to Bill Miller, but it hardly mattered. The Packers ran away with Super Bowl II, 33–14.

Once again Starr was named Most Valuable Player. He had completed 13 out of 24 passes for 202 yards and one touchdown. It wasn't his statistics that earned him the award, however; it was the way Starr brilliantly called the plays and kept the Raiders guessing. A year earlier he had

Nobody was happier than Vince Lombardi, the coach who had faith in Bart Starr.

outperformed Len Dawson, a veteran quarterback. Now he had gotten the better of Lamonica, a young man with a golden arm.

It was the perfect finale for Lombardi, who resigned as coach the next month.

Super Bowl III

Joe Namath
The Legend of Broadway Joe

It's a small town in western Pennsylvania, a place where men earn a living working in the coal mines and steel mills. It's a tough life, and for most, there is no escaping it. Like their fathers and grandfathers, boys in Beaver Falls grow up and follow the same dusty path.

But for some, sports can be a way out. When he was barely bigger than a football, Joe Namath was already being taught how to play the game by his two older brothers. In high school he was a football, baseball, and basketball star. More than 50 colleges wanted him to accept their football scholarships, and baseball's Chicago Cubs offered him a $50,000 bonus to sign.

Joe chose football. He became an All-America quarterback at Alabama and the number 1 draft choice of both the National and American Football Leagues.

In 1965, Namath signed with the New York Jets of the AFL for $400,000, a record contract at that time. The

*good-looking, dark-haired quarterback soon became a New
York celebrity. Everyone called him Broadway Joe.*

He swooped into Miami like one of the tropical storms
that threaten the city in late summer and early fall. The
weeks before the first two Super Bowls were calm compared
to the controversy Joe Namath stirred up before Super Bowl
III on January 12, 1969.

Namath was the swashbuckling quarterback of the New
York Jets, a 25-year-old bachelor who had two bad knees, a
strong arm, and, according to the Baltimore Colts, a big
mouth. Namath was outspoken, all right. All week long he
had been telling anyone who would listen that the Jets were
going to amaze everyone—the fans, the experts, and most of
all, the Colts. "We are going to win," he said. "I guarantee
it."

Most of the football experts thought Joe was crazy. The
Colts were big favorites to win. They had lost only one game
all season, then rolled to a 37–0 victory against the Cleveland Browns in the NFL title game. The Jets seemed an or-
dinary team, not even as good as the Oakland Raiders or the
Kansas City Chiefs, the AFL's first two Super Bowl repre-
sentatives.

"On Sunday, Joe Namath will play his first professional
game," said Otto Graham, a former All-Pro quarterback
with the Browns.

Namath spent the entire week getting in and out of trouble. He and teammates Emerson Boozer and Matt Snell
were fined for oversleeping on Picture Day—when the players pose in uniform for the photographers. Then Namath
was asked about Colt quarterback Earl Morrall, a veteran

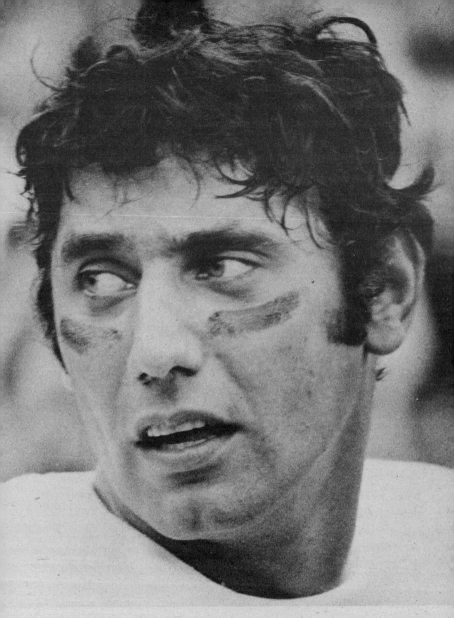

Joe Namath catches his breath on the sidelines after the New York Jets take an early lead over the Baltimore Colts in Super Bowl III.

who had filled in for the injured Johnny Unitas and taken the team to the NFL title.

"We've got four quarterbacks in our league who are better," the brash Namath said. "Even Babe Parilli, my substitute, is better than Morrall."

"I don't see how Namath can say that," said Don Shula, coach of the Colts. "We're happy with Earl."

Namath did not stop there. He had decided that the Raiders and the Chiefs had said too many nice things about the Green Bay Packers in the first two Super Bowls. They were awed by the Packers. Namath was building the confidence of his teammates. "That's just the way Joe is," said Jim Hudson, a defensive back for the Jets.

Namath even argued with Lou Michaels, the Colts' placekicker and brother of the Jets' defensive coach, Walt Michaels.

"We're going to beat the heck out of you," Namath told Michaels when they met in a restaurant.

"Haven't you heard of the word 'modesty'?" Michaels answered. But before the night was over, Namath paid for Michaels' dinner and drove him back to the Colts' hotel.

"He's not such a bad kid after all," Michaels said.

But on the morning of January 12 the Colts were ready to teach Joe Namath a lesson. "Let's give him some humility," defensive captain Billy Ray Smith told his teammates.

But Namath was still confident. "I feel loose," he said in the locker room. "Hey, guys, I feel so loose my arm feels like it's going to fall off." As Namath walked into the shower room to shave before the game, he sang his Beaver Falls High School fight song.

There were 75,377 people at the Orange Bowl that day waiting to see if Namath could back up his boasts. Before

21

the game started, the three astronauts who had circled the moon recited the Pledge of Allegiance. Then the teams came rushing out, the Jets led by Weeb Ewbank, the roly-poly coach who had taken the Colts to two NFL championships.

Right from the start both teams were able to move the football. The Colts drove 54 yards the first time they had the ball, as Morrall cleverly mixed his passes and running plays. When the Jet defense held at the 19-yard line, Lou Michaels attempted a 27-yard field goal. It should have been an easy kick for Lou—but somehow he missed. The Colts stared at one another in disbelief.

But the Colt offensive team had barely reached the sideline before it was time to return to the field. George Sauer, the Jets' talented wide receiver, had fumbled the ball after catching one of Namath's passes. The Colts had a first down on the Jets' 13-yard line as the first quarter ended.

Tom Matte took a handoff and raced around left end for seven yards. The Colts were at the six and closing in. Morrall dropped back to pass and spotted tight end Tom Mitchell alone in the end zone. He threw, and the ball bounced off Mitchell's hands and into the waiting arms of defensive back Randy Beverly. The Colts were foiled again. "Lucky, they're just lucky," Colt center Bill Curry muttered as he left the field.

Joe Namath knew an opportunity when he saw one. The Colts looked dejected. He took advantage of the situation. Playing like a veteran instead of an outspoken kid, he handed off to Matt Snell four times in a row as the Jets started to roll. Then, moving quickly on those gimpy knees and wearing his trademark white shoes, Broadway Joe began to throw the ball on target.

Soon the Jets were on the Colts' four-yard line. Snell took the handoff, and the big fullback thundered over the left side for a touchdown. The Jets were winning, 7–0. It was the first time an AFL team had ever held the lead in a Super Bowl.

The Colts were frustrated. Lou Michaels missed another field-goal attempt. Johnny Sample, a former Colt, intercepted one of Morrall's passes on the Jets' two-yard line. Then, just before halftime, the Colts tried a trick play from the Jets' 41. Morrall handed off to running back Tom Matte, who lateraled back to Morrall. Wide receiver Jimmy Orr was all alone in the end zone.

Morrall looked and looked and finally passed to Jerry Hill. Jim Hudson gave the Jets another interception.

At halftime the Colts were in shock.

"Didn't you see me?" Jimmy Orr screamed at Morrall as the teams left the field.

"No, I didn't," Morrall said in a whisper.

A furious Don Shula lectured the Colts during the break, but that didn't help much. At the start of the third quarter Matte fumbled and the Jets recovered. Namath was just 33 yards from another touchdown.

Now, however, he was playing conservatively. He was proving to be more than just a strong-armed quarterback. He moved the Jets into field-goal range, where Jim Turner kicked a 32-yarder to give New York a 10–0 lead.

Namath continued to work his magic when the Jets had the ball. Snell was battering the defense with his runs up the middle; Namath was picking apart the secondary with short passes to Sauer and Pete Lammons. With 3:58 remaining in the quarter, Turner kicked a 30-yard field goal. Incredibly, the Jets led, 13–0.

The Jets' Bill Mathis leads the interference for Matt Snell (41), who scored the first touchdown against the Colts.

Don Shula nervously paced the sidelines. "Earl, I'm going to make a change," he told Morrall. "We've got to try something." Johnny Unitas, an NFL legend, came off the bench, in spite of his injury, to lead the offense. But even Unitas could not budge the Jets.

Namath was having no problems with the Colt defense.

Twice he found George Sauer open, once for an 11-yard gain, the second time for 39 yards. As the Jets huddled, center John Schmitt could hear the Colts grumbling. "Hey, guys, they're cursing over there," he told his teammates. "They're mad because we're moving the ball."

By the start of the fourth quarter the Jets had moved to the two-yard line and Turner was trotting out to attempt another field goal. As Namath wandered to the sidelines, he realized that the game was almost won. How would he celebrate? Namath thought about the time Beaver Falls High School had won the league title in football. Joe had climbed up the flagpole on top of a building in town and tied an orange balloon around it. That had gotten him into plenty of trouble with the police.

That wasn't the first time Joe'd been in hot water. In fact, there were people in Beaver Falls who didn't think much of young Joe. They thought he was a wise guy, always talking back to his teachers. They thought his coach, Larry Bruno, was protecting him. Funny, but people still thought Namath was a wise guy.

As Namath watched from the sidelines, Turner kicked a nine-yard field goal to give the Jets a 16–0 lead. Unitas tried, but it was too late for the Colts. They scored a touchdown with 3:19 left to avoid a shutout.

The Jets had staged one of the biggest upsets in professional sports history. Led by their gifted quarterback, they had defeated the Colts, 16–7, proving that the AFL was the equal of the NFL.

Joe Namath, who'd completed 17 out of 28 passes for 206 yards, was named the Most Valuable Player.

"What I like about Joe," Weeb Ewbank said, "is that he is a winner. He doesn't know about losing."

Super Bowl IV

Len Dawson
Hail to the Chief

His teammates called him Lenny the Cool. It seemed that quarterback Len Dawson of the Kansas City Chiefs always had the situation under control. On and off the field Dawson was the quiet type, never one to raise his voice. He was not as showy as Joe Namath and he was not as highly thought of as Bart Starr, but he made the Chiefs winners anyway. "When you do something wrong, he just gives you that look and you know you better shape up," teammate Ed Budde said.

Dawson had spent five years on the bench with Pittsburgh and Cleveland in the NFL before getting his chance with the AFL's Chiefs. "I wasted those five years in the NFL," he said.

Dawson was not big for a quarterback, only 6 feet and 190 pounds, but he was an All-American in college at Purdue and became the number 1 draft choice of the Steelers.

Len grew up in Alliance, Ohio. He had six older brothers, and he felt he was forced to play football because they did.

"If I didn't go out for football," he said, "I couldn't have gone home. Actually, I should have been a golfer." As far as the Chiefs were concerned, golf's loss was their gain.

Practice was over, the interviews were done, and Len Dawson was resting in the privacy of his hotel room, away from all the attention a Super Bowl quarterback receives. It had been a difficult year for Len even though the Chiefs had won the AFL championship and were in New Orleans for their second Super Bowl. On January 11, 1970, they would face the Minnesota Vikings, champions of the NFL.

Dawson had played most of the season with a broken bone in his right hand that made it hard for him even to take the snap from center. He'd missed six games because of a knee injury too. Then, the night before the AFL title game against the Oakland Raiders, his father had died.

And now, before the biggest game of his career, there was more bad news. A television station had just reported that Len was friendly with a professional gambler who bet a lot of money on football games. Betting on football was illegal, and people wanted to know if Dawson was involved in it.

At a team breakfast meeting Len had told the Chiefs he was not involved in any illegal activities. His teammates had stood and applauded. Still, as he sat on his hotel bed trying to relax, his stomach churned.

"Len, this looks like it's eating you up inside," said his roommate, Johnny Robinson. "You look like you've aged five years this week."

The news was disturbing to Dawson's family as well. His wife, Jackie, kept Lenny, Jr., and Lisa home from school on Tuesday of Super Bowl Week and packed for an early trip to New Orleans. Lenny, Jr., who was 11 years old, did not want to go. He was afraid the fans would boo his father.

"Lenny," Mrs. Dawson told her son, "not everyone loves your daddy like we do. Now this is the biggest moment of his life and he wants to share it with you."

The Dawson family packed some warm clothes when they heard what the weather was like in New Orleans. This was the first Super Bowl to be played there and the last one between the AFL and NFL because the leagues were to merge the following season. Temperatures fell as low as 24 degrees, and the huge fountain outside the Chiefs' hotel froze.

On the day of the game the weather was wet and windy and there was a tornado warning for New Orleans. In spite of that, Len Dawson was feeling much better because he had been cleared of any involvement in the gambling case. All he had to worry about now were the Vikings, a rough-and-tumble football team whose defensive squad was known as the Purple People Eaters. The Vikings were big favorites to win Super Bowl IV.

Like the three previous Super Bowls, this one had a pre-game show. A man dressed as a Viking was supposed to sail across the field in a hot-air balloon to greet another man dressed as an Indian chief, riding in a balloon of his own. Instead, the Viking's balloon crashed into the stands. Luckily, no one was hurt. The Indian chief never got off the ground.

While all this was happening, the phone rang in the office of Hank Stram, the Chiefs' coach. "Hello," Stram said. . . . "Yes, Mr. President. . . . Thank you, sir."

President Richard Nixon had called from the White House to wish the Chiefs good luck, especially because of all the trouble they'd had during the week.

But it was obvious right from the start that Len Dawson was as confident as ever. The first time the Chiefs had the ball, Dawson directed them from the 17-yard line to the Vikings' 41. Jan Stenerud then kicked a 48-yard field goal—the longest ever kicked in a Super Bowl—to give the Chiefs a 3–0 lead.

No one was happier than the Chiefs' placekicker. Born in Oslo, Norway, Stenerud came to Montana State University on a skiing scholarship. He was 19 when he saw his first football. He began kicking for fun, but soon the Montana coaches saw how good he was.

"My parents still don't know what I do for a living," he said after he joined the Chiefs.

But the Vikings knew all too well. They were finding it difficult to break through the Chiefs' defense. Led by Buck Buchanan, Jerry Mays, and Willie Lanier, the Chiefs were much stronger than the Vikings had expected.

Early in the second quarter Dawson went to work again. Running back Mike Garrett tore through the Purple People Eaters time and time again while Dawson kept them off guard with his passing attack. When the drive was halted at the Vikings' 25, Stenerud kicked his second field goal to make the score 6–0.

The crowd of more than 80,000 in Tulane Stadium sat chilled by the wind and stunned by the Chiefs' domination. Was Kansas City going to repeat the AFL upset the Jets had scored the year before?

Even though the Chiefs were playing conservatively, they had a surprise or two for the Vikings. Wide receiver Frank Pitts took a handoff from Dawson on the end-around play and set up another field goal by Stenerud. This one gave the Chiefs a 9–0 lead.

It had been a horrible week for Kansas City's Len Dawson (16), but he was his cool self against Minnesota on the field.

After Stenerud kicked off, Charlie West fumbled, and the Chiefs recovered on the Vikings' 19-yard line. It took Dawson just five plays to move the Chiefs into the end zone—Garrett scored on a five-yard run.

The Chiefs led at halftime, 16–0, and Dawson ran off the field clapping his hands, an unusual show of emotion for the quiet quarterback.

"Just thirty minutes more," Hank Stram told his team in the locker room, "and we'll be world champions."

Meanwhile, on the field there was another entertainment disaster. The halftime show featured a re-creation of the Battle of New Orleans between the British and American soldiers, only this time the cannons were frightening the horses and the British seemed to be winning. History was not going to repeat itself.

The Vikings were determined to use all their cannons in the second half. They drove 69 yards to a touchdown in the third quarter with Dave Osborn running in from the four. Suddenly it was 16–7.

Len Dawson went back on the field, as calm as ever. He wasn't about to panic. He moved the Chiefs to the Vikings' 46-yard line, where he called a short pass play for flanker Otis Taylor.

Dawson dropped back, floated a short pass to Taylor, then watched in amazement as Taylor caught the ball, ran through Earsell Macbee, and was in the clear.

At the 20-yard line Karl Kassulke moved in to make the tackle, but Taylor speeded up and was gone. A simple pass play had become a 46-yard touchdown. Now the Chiefs led, 23–7, and the Vikings were demoralized.

There was very little excitement during the rest of the game. Dawson controlled the ball as the clock ran down and the Vikings watched helplessly. When the final gun sounded, the Chiefs had won Super Bowl IV, 23–7, and had gotten revenge for their loss to the Packers in the first Super Bowl.

In the locker room Len Dawson politely answered reporters' questions, but he rarely smiled. The problems he had had during that week would not be easy to forget. Still, he was voted the Most Valuable Player of the game after completing 12 out of 17 passes for one touchdown. He hugged Lenny, Jr., in celebration.

Then Dawson was told he had a telephone call. He walked into the coach's office and lifted the receiver. "Hello. . . . Yes, this is Len Dawson. . . . Thank you, Mr. President. I appreciate it."

Super Bowl V

Chuck Howley
A Prize for the Loser

Some of his teammates were bigger, others were faster, and most were flashier, the kind of players the fans can spot easily. But none of the Dallas Cowboys was more respected around the National Football League than Chuck Howley, who in his own quiet way had become one of the game's best linebackers.

For 12 years Howley had been a cornerstone in the Cowboys' "Doomsday Defense." He was a soft-spoken man, saying little on or off the field and rarely raising his voice. Opponents, however, quickly learned not to underestimate this broad-shouldered native of the West Virginia coal country.

Howley went to the University of West Virginia where he was a star not only in football, but in wrestling, track, swimming, and gymnastics. Playing five sports helped him develop a quickness and agility unusual for someone who was 6-foot-2 and weighed 225 pounds.

Howley was the number 1 draft choice of the Chicago Bears in 1958, but a knee injury slowed him down and the *impatient Bears released him. Two years later the Cowboys became the NFL's newest franchise and they traded a draft choice to Chicago for Howley. It proved a wise move. In 12 years Howley was named All-Pro seven times. Now, on January 17, 1971, he was leading the Cowboys into their first Super Bowl.*

Even for a veteran like Chuck Howley, who had been through two NFL title games and four conference championships, there was nothing quite like being in the Super Bowl.

Some people thought the Cowboys should have been there sooner. Since 1966 Dallas had won more games than any other team in the NFL. But the Cowboys always seemed to fall just short of winning the game that would put them ahead of everyone else. Finally, in 1970, after a slow start, they had come through to win the National Football Conference title and earn a trip to Super Bowl V in Miami, where they would face the Baltimore Colts, the American Football Conference champions.

Before then, Howley had begun to think he would never have a chance to play in a Super Bowl. He was 34 years old and relying more on experience than on the physical strength he'd had as a younger player. "Better late than never," he figured. After all, his pro career had almost ended before it started.

He thought back to 1958 when he had injured his knee and undergone surgery. The Bears had given up on Howley then and he had gone home to Wheeling, West Virginia, where he worked at a service station pumping gas. "I didn't have a penny," he said. "I wondered what was going to become of me."

For Howley, a chance to perform in the Super Bowl was worth all the hard times. He and the rest of the Cowboys were eager to make the most of this opportunity. The Colts were here for revenge, however. They had first come to Miami for Super Bowl III, when they'd been embarrassed by Joe Namath and the Jets.

Colt quarterback Earl Morrall had nightmares about that Jets game for two years. All he could remember were the bad things. When the Colts' plane arrived in Miami for Super Bowl V, Morrall stepped off and said: "Well, here I am at the scene of the crime. There is no way I can ever escape it."

So both the Cowboys and the Colts felt they had something to prove. The teams were equally matched in this first Super Bowl played since the AFL and NFL merged. In the new lineup of teams, all but three of the old NFL teams wound up in the National Football Conference. The exceptions were the Cleveland Browns, the Pittsburgh Steelers, and the Baltimore Colts. Those three teams joined the AFL teams in the American Football Conference to make 12 teams in each conference. The Colts were bitter about having to join the AFL teams. When asked how they could identify with them, veteran defensive tackle Billy Ray Smith said, "We're here to win for the Colts, no one else."

Namath's performance two years earlier had helped make Super Bowl V an especially exciting sports event. There was a crowd of 80,055 in the Orange Bowl on a beautiful warm Sunday afternoon. After the national anthem was played and Air Force jets roared overhead, rookie Jim O'Brien prepared to kick off for the Colts.

Though the Colts had an excellent defense the Cowboy defense was even tougher. During the second half of the season and in two playoff games, it had allowed just one touchdown.

With a first down on his 47-yard line, Johnny Unitas, the aging Colt quarterback who was still one of the best in the game, tried to lob a soft pass to running back Norm Bulaich. As the ball floated above him like a balloon, Chuck Howley displayed some of the agility he had developed in college. He leaped high and tipped the ball with his hand, then lunged forward and caught it just before it hit the ground. Interception, Dallas.

The Cowboys could not move the ball, but they got a break when Colt Ron Gardin fumbled Ron Widby's punt at his own nine-yard line. The Cowboys got nowhere on the next three plays. In fact, they were pushed back to the Colt 14. That was an ideal spot for Mike Clark, who kicked a field goal, giving Dallas a 3–0 lead.

Early in the second quarter, quarterback Craig Morton led the Cowboys on a long drive that resulted in another field goal by Clark. Now it was 6–0.

Unitas, meanwhile, was frustrated. Two passes fell incomplete as Howley and the rest of the Dallas defense kept the pressure on him. On the third down from his 25-yard line, Unitas was rushed again and threw a hurried pass too high for Eddie Hinton, who was able only to tip it with his fingers.

Mel Renfro, the Cowboys' cornerback, tried to intercept the pass before it hit the ground. But he, too, was able to just touch it with his fingers. Then, amazingly, there was Colt tight end John Mackey several yards downfield, ready to snatch the pass. He caught it and ran all the way for a touchdown. The strange play covered 75 yards.

Chuck Howley, leader of the Dallas "Doomsday Defense," made two interceptions against Baltimore, one here on a Johnny Unitas pass.

Jim O'Brien's extra-point attempt was blocked, and the score was tied, 6–6.

The Cowboys' defense did not let that touchdown pass bother it. "Lee Roy, let's you and me blitz on this play," Howley said to teammate Lee Roy Jordan, guessing that Unitas would pass.

It was third down and long yardage and the Colts were on their 21. Howley figured right. He and Jordan hit Unitas at the same time, and the quarterback fumbled the ball. Jethro Pugh recovered for Dallas at the Colts' 28.

Three plays later Morton threw a seven-yard touchdown pass to Duane Thomas, and the Cowboys led, 13–6.

Howley and his teammates were not through with Unitas. They hit him so hard as he attempted to pass that the ball was intercepted by Renfro, and Unitas had to leave the game because of a sore shoulder. But Morton could not move the ball, and by halftime the score was still 13–6.

The Cowboys were clearly in control, however. In the third quarter they marched to the Colts' two-yard line. Duane Thomas took the handoff and was almost in the end zone when he was hit by Jerry Logan. Fumble. The Colts recovered.

The Cowboy defense held firm. Earl Morrall, now at quarterback, marched the Colts to the 11-yard line, where he fired a pass to Bulaich in the end zone.

Touchdown? No! Chuck Howley stepped in front of the receiver and made his second interception of the game. The defense had held again. But not forever.

Craig Morton was having his own problems with the Colts. One of his passes was picked off by Rick Volk, who ran it down to the Cowboys' two-yard line. This time there was nothing Howley could do as fullback Tom Nowatzke

The Colts' Jim O'Brien leaps to the sky after kicking the field goal that meant victory in the Super Bowl.

dove in for the touchdown. With only seven minutes left, the score was tied at 13–13.

Was the Super Bowl about to have its first sudden-death overtime? It seemed that way. Morton threw a pass that bounced off running back Dan Reeves's hands and was intercepted by Mike Curtis of the Colts.

The crowd was on its feet, cheering loudly, making it difficult for the Colts to hear Morrall's signals. Cautiously, Morrall moved the Colts into field-goal range and called a time-out with nine seconds to go. The ball was on the Cowboys' 32-yard line. Jim O'Brien ran onto the field.

"Be cool, kid, be cool," Morrall told the rookie kicker. "Just keep your head down and kick it."

The ball was snapped and Morrall placed it down. O'Brien thrust his right foot forward, staring at the ball and never looking up. "It feels good," he thought. "I hit it good. I know I did."

O'Brien was right. When he looked up, the ball was soaring over the crossbar like a proud bird. The field goal was good and the Colts were jumping into O'Brien's arms. They had won Super Bowl V, 16–13.

On the sidelines Craig Morton hung his head. "Why is this happening?" he muttered. Bob Lilly threw his helmet and Chuck Howley slumped over. A great defensive performance had been wasted.

But the sportswriters appreciated Howley's efforts. He was named the Most Valuable Player of the game, the first one chosen from a losing team. Howley was thankful, but disappointed too. "I'd rather be the champion," he said. "I won't be satisfied until we are. We'll be back."

Super Bowl VI

Roger Staubach
Year of the Cowboy

Even when he was growing up in the Cincinnati suburb of Silverton, Ohio, Roger Staubach showed that he was a very determined young man. Whether he was playing baseball, basketball, or football, Roger was never satisfied unless he won. "I wasn't the hot-tempered type, though," he said. "But I enjoyed being in the middle of things."

There might have been others who had more talent but none who wanted to succeed as much as Staubach. He won nine letters in high school and received 25 football scholarship offers from such schools as Michigan, Purdue, and Ohio State. Notre Dame was his first choice, but it offered him only a basketball scholarship. So Roger chose the Naval Academy at Annapolis, Maryland. He was the starting quarterback as a sophomore, and he won the Heisman Trophy as the country's best collegian in his junior year. He was an All-America player and the all-American boy. He was a dazzling, scrambling quarterback who captured the imagination of football fans around the country.

Because he had to serve four years in the Navy after graduation, most observers felt Staubach would never play professional football. The Dallas Cowboys made him a tenth-round draft pick in 1964, however, and in 1969, as a 27-year-old civilian, he became a rookie quarterback in the NFL. Two years later he replaced Craig Morton as the starter and led the Cowboys to their second Super Bowl in a row. As champions of the National Football Conference, they would meet the Miami Dolphins, champions of the American Football Conference, on January 16, 1972, at Tulane Stadium in New Orleans.

Roger Staubach ducked his head into the huddle and waited for the messenger guard to bring in the next play from coach Tom Landry. Staubach blew on his hands to keep them warm in the unusually cold New Orleans air. Even the best professional quarterbacks usually don't get to decide on what play to call. That decision lies with the coach—in this case, Landry.

It was the first period, and the Cowboys were on the move. They were on the Miami Dolphins' 18-yard line, third down with four yards to go. This was Staubach's second Super Bowl, but the year before he had been only a spectator watching from the bench. This was different—and the excitement shot through him like a lightning bolt.

Staubach called Landry's play and followed center Dave Manders to the line of scrimmage. There were 81,023 fans in the stands, and many were cheering now, expecting the Cowboys to score. Staubach took the snap and quickly dropped back to pass. He spotted running back Duane Thomas and fired a short, hard pass; Thomas caught it like a spider trapping a fly.

Thomas spun and twisted for five more yards before the Dolphins' Tim Foley tackled him. The Cowboys had another first down, this time at the seven-yard line.

Two running plays moved the ball to the four, and then Staubach threw another short pass to Thomas. The Dolphins were waiting, though, and defensive back Dick Anderson moved in quickly to stop Thomas for no gain. Now it was fourth down and the Cowboys were two yards from the end zone. Landry decided not to gamble and sent in Mike Clark to attempt a field goal.

Staubach trotted off the field, a little disappointed but looking forward to trying again. Playing quarterback is the most glamorous job in football, but there was a time when Staubach did not think so. He was a teenager then, attending Purcell High, a Catholic school in Cincinnati. On the day coach Jim McCarthy moved Staubach from wide receiver to quarterback, Roger came home crying.

"He didn't like it at all," said his mother, Betty Staubach. "Purcell wasn't a school where the quarterback ran." And how Roger Staubach loved to run. Here, there, everywhere on a football field.

By the time he was a senior in high school, he was one of the most exciting players in the country. Staubach would drop back to pass, then begin to run in that razzle-dazzle style of his. "Only God and Roger know what he's going to do," said a Navy coach scouting Staubach.

Staubach brought that same style to Navy and made it famous. But coach Landry didn't like to see Staubach running all over the field. "I guess I give him a few gray hairs," Staubach said.

Mike Clark's field-goal attempt from nine yards away was good. The Cowboys had taken the lead, 3–0, with one minute remaining in the first quarter of Super Bowl VI. Maybe this would finally be their day. The Cowboys had become one of the finest teams in the NFL, but they never seemed to be able to win the championship. This year they had come to New Orleans a very determined team, but it was obvious the pressure was on them more than the Dolphins.

The Dolphins were in only their sixth year of existence, but a combination of good draft picks and the coaching of Don Shula had carried them to the top in a hurry.

It was a young team, and not many of the players were well known, especially those on defense. Quarterback Bob Griese was a lot like Staubach—a quiet, modest individual who came from the Midwest and was a devoted family man. The Dolphins' offense revolved around Griese's passing to Paul Warfield, and the running of Larry Csonka and Jim Kiick, who were not fancy or fast but a couple of tough ball carriers who worked hard for every yard they got.

As the game entered the second quarter the yards were especially hard to get for the Dolphins. The Cowboys' defense had smothered them. The closest they came to scoring was a 49-yard field-goal attempt by Garo Yepremian that fell short.

Then, with 6:15 remaining in the first half, Staubach launched another Cowboy drive. He made Duane Thomas his workhorse, giving him the ball on three running plays, then tossing him a short pass to pick up a first down. The Cowboys had moved from their 24 to the 46.

Thomas was one of the best running backs in the NFL but a mystery man otherwise. Because of a contract dispute with management, he refused to speak to reporters, coaches, or his teammates. Instead, he let his actions speak for him.

The Dolphins were so preoccupied with trying to stop

Thomas that they forgot about the rest of the Cowboys. Staubach found Lance Alworth open and the pass play gained 21 yards. Then Calvin Hill, a Yale graduate and Thomas' running mate, broke loose for gains of 13 and seven yards, giving the Cowboys a second and three at the Miami 12-yard line. Once again it was Hill running around left end for five more yards and a first down. Then Staubach drilled a pass to Alworth for the first touchdown of the game. The Cowboys led, 10–0.

There was just a minute remaining in the half, and the Cowboys' defense relaxed. Griese took advantage, driving the Dolphins into field-goal range. Yepremian kicked a 31-yarder to make it 10–3 at halftime.

It was obvious that the Dolphins were going to have to do something drastic in order to win. Their lack of experience was showing. At halftime Shula searched for the answers, even giving some thought to the play President Richard Nixon had suggested to him the week before.

It had been late at night and Shula was sleeping when Nixon called from the White House. "At first I thought it was a nut," said Shula, who was accustomed to receiving crank calls. But it was the President, who just wanted to chat about football—and suggest a pass play for Warfield.

The Cowboys got no such help. And many people figured that Tom Landry did not need any. The team had gotten off to a slow start during the regular season, losing three of its first seven games. Then Landry benched Craig Morton and gave the quarterback job to Staubach. The Cowboys closed out the season by winning nine games in a row. "Roger is unusual," Landry said. "He has the traits to make a good quarterback and the dedication to do it. He wants to be the top man."

Dallas' Roger Staubach was often referred to as "Roger the Dodger," and that's what he is here against Miami in Super Bowl VI.

Even if he wasn't calling his own plays, Staubach was a leader on the field. At the start of the third quarter he discouraged the Dolphins' defense with another long drive, beginning at his 29-yard line. When Staubach wasn't completing a pass, he was handing off to Thomas, who slashed through the Dolphins for big gains, including a 23-yarder that put the ball on the Miami 22.

Three plays later Staubach again handed off to Thomas,

who ran three yards for a touchdown. The Cowboys led, 17–3. They were beginning to sense it now on the sidelines: They were playing too well to lose this time. All those years of coming close were just one quarter away from being forgotten.

Staubach thought about his days in the Navy and the year he spent as a supply officer in Vietnam. Although there was a war on, he continued to run and throw a football every day, dreaming of playing for the Cowboys. In 1966 he wrote a letter to Gil Brandt, the team's director of player personnel, and asked him for a new football. "The rough terrain in Vietnam wore mine out," Staubach wrote. Brandt sent him a football. It was a wise investment.

Now, after missing those four years and then playing two more in the shadows as Morton's substitute, Staubach had emerged as a star.

In the fourth quarter, after linebacker Chuck Howley intercepted a Griese pass and returned it to the nine-yard line, Staubach made good use of the opportunity. He threw a seven-yard touchdown pass to Mike Ditka. The Cowboys had increased their lead to 24–3.

On the sidelines Dolphin linebacker Nick Buoniconti sat dazed after taking a blow to the head. "What's the score?" he asked teammate Bob Matheson.

"Twenty-four to three," was the answer.

"I thought it was only ten to three," Buoniconti said.

Any chance the Dolphins had to make a comeback ended when Staubach used up seven minutes on a long drive that would have resulted in another touchdown if Calvin Hill had not fumbled at the one-yard line. Instead it served to run out the clock and give the Cowboys their first Super Bowl victory. The final score: 24–3.

And Roger Staubach, Navy man and all-American boy, was named the Most Valuable Player of the game. He'd completed 12 out of 19 passes for 119 yards and two touchdowns. "This is what I've been looking forward to," he said. "This is what I wanted to prove to myself."

Super Bowl VII

Jake Scott
Great Scott!

He grew up in Athens, Georgia, home of the University of Georgia. As a young man, Jake Scott liked to ride across the red clay of the Georgia countryside on a minibike. He admits he spent just about as much time shooting pool as he did attending high-school classes. He was a good athlete, though, and he played for a team coached by Fran Tarkenton, the same Fran Tarkenton who would become an outstanding quarterback in the NFL.

Jake and his family eventually moved to Arlington, Virginia, but he returned to Athens as a student at the university. He wanted to be a wide receiver, but coach Vince Dooley made him a defensive back. And he was still a free spirit. He seemed to be involved in every water fight in the dormitories.

Scott's college career came to an end after the 1969 season when he still had a year of eligibility remaining. He decided to turn professional and sign a one-year contract with the British Columbia Lions of the Canadian Football

League. A lot of people at Georgia were upset, but Jake was doing what he thought was best for him. In 1970 he was drafted by the Miami Dolphins. He left Canada because he wanted to play in the best league there was—the NFL.

It was a short kick but very high, and Jake Scott thought the ball would never come down. He could hear the pounding of feet as the Washington Redskins came thundering toward him, getting closer and closer. Still, Scott was in no mood to signal for a fair catch. It just wasn't his style. He was going to make a run for it.

Finally he could see the laces of the football as it tumbled into his hands. He took one step, then another, and was hit by the Redskins' Ted Vactor. The ball squirted from Scott's hands as he fell. What a time to fumble!

It was January 14, 1973, and the Washington Redskins of the NFC and the Miami Dolphins of the AFC were in Super Bowl VII before a crowd of 90,182 at the Los Angeles Coliseum.

Fortunately for Scott and the Dolphins, teammate Dick Anderson fell on the loose ball. But as Scott trotted off the field he wondered whether he had made a mistake in trying to play. For two weeks before the game he had been unable to practice because of a shoulder separation suffered during the playoffs. His shoulder still felt sore, but this wasn't the first time Scott had played with an injury. It seemed normal for him.

In fact, the year before, Jake had played in Super Bowl VI against the Cowboys with two broken wrists. A couple of weeks later he went skiing in Colorado with both hands in casts. "As long as you don't fall down," he said, "you don't have any trouble." As long as Jake Scott could walk, he would try to play.

On the sidelines teammates patted him on the back and told him to forget about the fumble. The Dolphins had recovered it, and now they were moving down the field against the Redskins. First, running back Jim Kiick had set the defense on its heels with a couple of hard runs that gained 11 yards. Then quarterback Bob Griese found Paul Warfield open and completed a 14-yard pass. First down on the Washington 34-yard line.

These were the same Dolphins who had been beaten so badly by the Cowboys in Super Bowl VI. But like most teams making a second appearance in football's biggest game, they had learned from their first experience. The Dolphins had come to Los Angeles relaxed and confident that they would complete a perfect season. They had already won 16 games in a row.

Griese took the snap and tucked the ball into Larry Csonka's belly. The slow but bruising fullback lowered his head and gained a couple of hard-earned yards. Then his running mate Kiick slashed through the Redskins for some more yardage off left guard. Third down and four at the Washington 28-yard line.

On the next play Griese dropped back to pass and spotted Howard Twilley open at the five-yard line. Griese threw and Twilley caught the ball, then dashed into the end zone. The Dolphins were ahead, 7–0.

Coach Don Shula clapped his hands, but he looked worried. There were three more quarters to play. Shula had been the coach at Baltimore when the Colts lost to the Jets in Super Bowl III, the most memorable one so far. And he'd

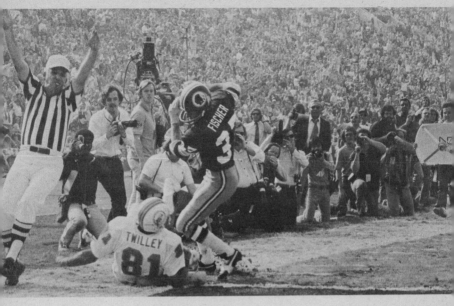

The Dolphins' Howard Twilley scores on a pass from Bob Griese.

been coaching when the Dolphins lost to the Cowboys in Super Bowl VI.

People had said Shula couldn't win the really big games. He felt such comments were unfair. The night before Super Bowl VII he'd stood on the balcony outside his hotel room, tired, nervous, and unable to sleep. His wife, Dorothy, held his hand. "Don't worry, Don, this time we're going to win," she said. "I know it."

The Redskins were making their first appearance in the Super Bowl. And even though this was a veteran team, the players and coach George Allen seemed upset by all the distractions in Los Angeles. "Too many reporters," Allen grumbled.

The team had practiced at Anaheim Stadium. On the first day 5,000 fans were allowed in free to watch. When practice ended, they charged onto the field looking for autographs. The Redskins escaped into the locker room. "I thought they might step on the players and break their legs," Allen said.

Now it was the Dolphins and their "no name" defense (they weren't stars with names everybody knew) that were making life miserable for the Redskins. Larry Brown and Charlie Harraway were stopped after one-yard gains. It was obvious that Washington quarterback Billy Kilmer would have to pass.

Kilmer dropped back and tossed one of those wobbly passes he had made famous during the season. It floated too far and almost went over everyone's head. But Jake Scott managed to get a hand on it, batting it up in the air. Then he made the interception and returned it eight yards before he was tackled. "I was lucky, I was lucky," Jake shouted as he ran happily off the field.

The defensive struggle continued as the crowd sat waiting for something to happen. Late in the second quarter something did. The Redskins had just crossed midfield when Kilmer attempted another pass. This time middle linebacker Nick Buoniconti made the interception and returned the ball 32 yards to the Washington 27. With 1:51 remaining in the half, the Dolphins were ready to score.

As usual it was Csonka and Kiick, chewing up yardage inside. Then Griese spotted Bob Mandich and completed a 19-yard pass to his tight end. First down on the two-yard line.

Only 46 seconds were left in the half, but Griese took his time. He handed off to Kiick, once, then again—the second

Miami's Jake Scott intercepted a Billy Kilmer pass in the end zone and ran it out 55 yards to stop a threat by Washington.

time for a touchdown from the one. At halftime the Dolphins were ahead, 14–0.

No one said much in the locker room. The Dolphins were not a bunch of colorful personalities. And even Scott, a reckless and exciting player on the field, treasured his peace and quiet off it. He loved skiing and living in the mountains where the winter snow muffles all sounds, far away from cities. Jake's favorite place was Colorado, and he was going to build a home there. "All I want to do is play football and be left alone," he said.

It might have been boring for the fans at the Coliseum and the millions watching on television, but Super Bowl VII was becoming the best defensive exhibition played so far. Neither team was able to move the ball in the third quarter. And it seemed unlikely that the Redskins would threaten when they took over at their 11-yard line early in the final period.

Unexpectedly, however, Kilmer had them on the move. The Redskins advanced mostly on the ground with Brown and Harraway carrying or Kilmer scrambling for a first down. They were at the Dolphins' 10-yard line when Kilmer dropped back to pass.

He was looking for Charley Taylor in the end zone. Taylor had apparently beaten his man, Lloyd Mumphord. But Jake Scott ran from his free safety position to help out Mumphord. Scott jumped in front of Taylor and intercepted the pass, carrying it 55 yards out of the end zone.

The defense was still celebrating on the sidelines as Griese moved the offense into field-goal range. Then came one of the strangest plays in the brief history of the Super Bowl. Garo Yepremian, the short, balding placekicker from the island of Cyprus, came onto the field to attempt a 42-yarder. His kick was low, however, and bounced off several players.

Yepremian scooped up the ball and tried to throw a pass. But the ball slipped out of his hand and was caught by the Redskins' Dick Bass. In a shocking play that brought new life to the slow-moving game, Bass ran 49 yards for a touchdown. The Redskins had finally scored. With two minutes left they now trailed, 14–7.

With 1:14 still showing on the clock, they got another chance, starting at their 30-yard line. Kilmer went back to pass, but twice his throws fell incomplete. Just 1:04 to go. Kilmer dropped back again and tossed a short pass to Larry

Brown. But Brown was tackled for a four-yard loss.

Fourth down and 42 seconds remained. Now Kilmer was looking for a receiver. He waited, but no one could break free. In fact, Kilmer waited too long. Soon the quarterback tumbled to the ground after being hit by defensive end Bill Stanfill. Time ran out—and the Dolphins had done it. They'd won the Super Bowl, 14–7, finishing a perfect season.

Because of his two interceptions and fine work overall, Jake Scott was named the game's Most Valuable Player. "Now I hope people will know who we are," he said.

Larry Csonka
Field Day for Zonk

When Larry Csonka was a youngster, his mother called him the Wonder because he always wanted to know what was on the other side of the street. Larry was born on Christmas Day, 1946, one of six Csonka children living with their parents on a small farm. Actually, there weren't many streets to be seen in Stow, Ohio, but Larry was a curious sort, and a little mischievous too.

It seems that Larry and his friends liked to tease the farmers, older kids, and sometimes even the police. "We used to throw snowballs at the police cars so they would stop and the cops would chase us into the woods," Csonka says. He enjoyed the thrill of a chase, a quality he says all running backs must have. There is nothing like escaping for a big gain or a touchdown.

Larry Csonka escaped many defensive players in his years at Syracuse University, where he became an All-America running back. He broke the school rushing record, which wasn't easy because Syracuse had turned out such excellent runners as *Jimmy Brown, Ernie Davis, Floyd Little,* and *Jim Nance.*

Larry was drafted by the Miami Dolphins. Soon he became the most feared fullback in the NFL, a bruising runner who was not fancy, but got the job done. Now, on January 13, 1974, he was leading the Dolphins to another Super Bowl appearance—against the Minnesota Vikings at Rice Stadium in Houston.

Larry Csonka placed his fingers carefully on the bridge of his nose. When he took them away, he saw they were covered with blood. The game had barely begun and Csonka's nose—the one he had broken so often in the past—already had a souvenir of Super Bowl VIII. It did not matter. If Csonka took a beating during a game, then at least he was one of the few running backs around who was capable of punishing the defense too. He felt his nose one last time, then listened to quarterback Bob Griese call the next play.

The big fullback had just rumbled through the Minnesota defense for 16 yards and a first down on the Vikings' 27-yard line. The Dolphins had taken the opening kickoff and were already threatening to score. Griese dropped back to pass and connected with wide receiver Marlon Briscoe for six yards. Csonka rumbled up the middle for five more yards and another first down. Now Miami was on the Vikings' 16.

Griese turned to Csonka again, and Larry gained eight more yards, dragging several Vikings with him. Mercury Morris added another three yards, and the Dolphins were on the five. First and goal.

The Viking defense braced, and Csonka knew the yards would be coming even harder. Still, he loved to try. "Running up the middle is like being a sneak thief," he once said.

"It's like you're stealing yardage. You're defying the defense and getting away with it."

Griese barked the signals and then handed off to Csonka. Larry lowered his head and slammed off right guard, slowing down only after he had reached the end zone. The Dolphins had scored on their first drive. They led, 7–0.

It was strange how the football experts did not seem to want to give the Dolphins the credit they deserved. Although there had not been many Super Bowls, Miami was the first team to play in three of them. And the Dolphins had done it three years in a row.

Maybe it was because Miami was a quiet and confident team with no heroes as big as Joe Namath or Bart Starr. Whatever the reason, the Dolphins kept having to prove themselves. And even though they had arrived in Houston as the favorites, maybe, just maybe, the experts thought, the Vikings would win.

There were 68,142 fans in Rice Stadium, however, who were beginning to wonder whether the Vikings even belonged there. The second time the Dolphins got the ball, they again took control. Griese swung a pass to Jim Mandich and the play gained eight yards. Morris and Csonka kept pounding at the Vikings' middle, picking up several yards at a time. Then Csonka made a rare run around the defense and picked up 12 yards. On the next play he went back through familiar territory, gaining eight yards off right guard. Miami was on the Vikings' 14-yard line.

Larry was breathing heavier now, feeling just a little tired. But he was showing the Vikings he was more than just a big moose playing in the backfield.

At his Florida retirement home Ben Schwartzwalder, Larry's old Syracuse coach, was enjoying the game on television. "When I first saw Larry, I couldn't believe the size of his neck," Schwartzwalder remembered. "Then, while we were talking, he saw a rabbit in the field and took off after it. He caught it too. 'What strength! What quickness!' I thought. I was planning to make this farmboy a linebacker."

Now Alan Page and Carl Eller, the Vikings' defensive linemen, wished that Larry had stayed on the farm. They thought Larry was going to take a handoff from Griese, but it was a fake. Griese dropped back and threw a 13-yard pass to Briscoe. The Dolphins were on the one-yard line. Two plays later Jim Kiick dove into the end zone for the touch-

Minnesota couldn't contain Miami's Larry Csonka (39), who set a Super Bowl record for yards gained—145.

down. The score was 14–0, and the Dolphins looked un-beatable.

Bud Grant, the Vikings' coach, paced up and down the sidelines. Minnesota's Fran Tarkenton was one of the most exciting quarterbacks in the NFL, but the way the Dolphins were controlling the football, Grant wondered whether Tarkenton would ever get a chance to show what he could do.

This was Minnesota's second trip to the Super Bowl. The Vikings had lost to Kansas City in Super Bowl IV, and this trip had gotten off to an even worse start. On the bus ride from the Houston airport to the hotel, one bus caught fire and broke down and the other got lost.

The Vikings did not have the best place to practice for the Super Bowl either. It was an old high-school field and the locker room was cramped and dirty. One day a flock of sparrows flew through it. "This is shabby treatment," Grant had said angrily. "This is the Super Bowl, not a pickup game."

But nothing was as shabby as the way the Dolphins were treating the Vikings. While the Minnesota offense remained stalled, Griese and Csonka continued to move almost at will. Midway through the second quarter the Dolphins scored again. Garo Yepremian connected on a 28-yard field goal, giving Miami a 17–0 lead. And the one time the Vikings threatened before the first half ended, running back Oscar Reed fumbled on the Dolphins' six-yard line.

If it weren't for the fact that this was the Super Bowl, some of the fans might have left at halftime. No wonder the Dolphins were so underrated. They seemed to bore their opponents to death. But Griese was only taking advantage of what was working best. He did not have to pass as much as in previous games. When Jake Scott returned a punt 12 yards to give his team good field position early in the third quarter, it was "The Larry Csonka Show" again.

As he'd been doing all day, Griese threw a pass only when the defense least expected it. This time he found Paul Warfield open on a 27-yard play, the longest gain of the day. Mostly, though, it was the player the Dolphins called Zonk, smashing up the middle for well-earned yards.

On the sidelines coach Don Shula looked more relaxed than he ever had during a game. "Larry is an old-fashioned player," he said. "He doesn't like to practice, but he is mean and tough in the games."

Csonka was 6-foot-2 and 237 pounds. With his nose flattened because of all those breaks, he looked very threatening. During Super Bowl Week a little girl slowly approached Csonka to ask for an autograph. She looked frightened. That bothered Larry. "I don't have fangs," he said. "I don't eat raw meat. I'm not big and dumb. I like kids and I enjoy talking to people."

Now, Csonka was doing his best to threaten the Vikings. He busted loose for six yards and a first down on Minnesota's two-yard line. How were the Vikings going to keep him out of the end zone this time? Griese called a play in the huddle, clapped his hands, and brought the Dolphins to the line of scrimmage. But a funny thing happened. The quarterback forgot the snap count. He turned and quietly asked Csonka, "What are we snapping on?"

"Uh, on one, no, it's two . . . no, four, uh, no, it's one," Csonka said.

Now Griese was even more confused. He looked at Kiick, who could not remember either. So he turned back to center Jim Langer and began calling signals: "Hut one, hut . . ."

Surprise! The ball was snapped on one. Griese calmly

handed it to Csonka, who slammed two yards for the touchdown. The Dolphins had taken a commanding 24–0 lead. There was more than a quarter and a half left to play, but the game was in effect over. The Vikings knew it too. "I've never seen anyone play fullback like that," Fran Tarkenton told his teammates on the sidelines. "But it must be normal for Csonka."

When the game ended, the Dolphins were the winners, 24–7. It was their second Super Bowl victory, and now some people were saying they might be the best team of all time. Larry Csonka certainly was one of the finest fullbacks. He'd gained 145 yards on 33 carries to set a Super Bowl record, and scored two touchdowns in the process. And nobody disagreed when he was chosen MVP of Super Bowl VIII.

Franco Harris
He Leads an Army

They met in Italy during the last days of World War II. She was Gina Parenti, a 17-year-old Italian who did not speak English; he was Cad Harris, a black American serving in the army as a medic. Neither color nor a language barrier could stand in the way of their love, though, and Cad Harris brought his Italian bride home with him to the United States. They settled in New Jersey and raised nine children. One of them was Franco Harris.

Franco was a quiet boy who made the high-school All-America team in his senior year at Rancocas Valley High in Mt. Holly, New Jersey. He went on to Penn State, where some people thought he did not live up to his high-school reputation. Coach Joe Paterno used him mostly as a blocker for Lydell Mitchell, Franco's flashier running mate.

But the Pittsburgh Steelers thought Franco could be an even better professional player than Mitchell. They drafted Harris on the first round in 1972, passing up an opportunity to take Mitchell. Franco did not let them down. He gained more than 1,000 yards in his first NFL season and quickly became a favorite of the long-suffering Steelers' fans. In his third season he led the Steelers to the playoffs, and now he and his teammates had made it to the Super Bowl for the first time. They would play the Minnesota Vikings in New Orleans on January 12, 1975.

The locker room was quiet. Some players sat resting against their lockers while others moved around, trying to walk off their nervousness. It had been a grueling first half, dominated by the defensive teams. Franco Harris was waiting for the halftime show to end, knowing full well that the Steelers' 2–0 lead was not going to be nearly enough.

They had scored when Viking quarterback Fran Tarkenton fumbled in the end zone. He recovered but was tackled for a safety. The Steelers' offense had moved into scoring range only once, with Harris doing most of the work from his fullback position. But a field-goal attempt backfired when the snap from center was too high. So here were the young Steelers, wondering whether they were capable of scoring a touchdown against the veteran Vikings.

Winning the Super Bowl would mean $15,000 per player, but that wasn't the Steelers' only incentive. They wanted to win the championship for Art Rooney, their 73-year-old owner, who had been one of the founding fathers of the NFL. In 42 years Rooney had never had a championship team.

"The Steelers have waited forty-two years to get here," Joe Greene, Franco's teammate, said in a pregame speech. "If we lose, it might be another forty-two before we get back. I don't expect to be playing that long. And let's win this for Mr. Rooney. He doesn't want to wait that long either."

Suddenly it was time to head for the field again. Time to continue this latest Battle of New Orleans. It was cold and windy in Tulane Stadium, but neither team seemed to mind.

Harris was on the sideline watching Roy Gerela kick off to the Vikings. As Gerela approached the ball, however, he lost his footing. It was almost funny to see him slip and fall as the ball popped into the air. It was a short kick, and the Vikings' Bill Brown moved up and caught it on the 30-yard line. He took two more steps before he was met by the on-rushing Steelers. Brown hit the ground and the ball rolled free. Fumble.

What a break for the Steelers! Their fans from Pittsburgh, wearing black and yellow and waving little flags, were screaming because their team had recovered. It was first down on the Minnesota 30.

Quarterback Terry Bradshaw was not going to rush into something foolish, though. He handed off to Rocky Bleier, who was stopped for no gain. Then Bradshaw faked to Bleier and gave the ball to Harris. Franco spotted a hole off the left side and burst through like an express train. He was 6-foot-2 and 230 pounds of speed and power. The Vikings did not catch him until he was on their six-yard line. First down and goal to go.

On the next play Harris tried to go around right end and was tackled for a three-yard loss. With second down on the nine, everyone figured Bradshaw would have to pass. "How do you feel, Franco?" the quarterback asked in the huddle.

"I'm all right," Harris said.

Bradshaw had a surprise for the Vikings. Instead of passing, he pitched the ball to Harris again, and this time the big fullback swept around the left side of the line, rumbling all the way into the end zone. The Steelers were ahead, 9–0.

Their fans were overjoyed. And the fans who called themselves Franco's Italian Army waved their flags and shouted his name. At this moment, as he had been all season, Franco Harris was the most popular man in Pittsburgh. And New Orleans.

All the fame, however, never seemed to change him. Annette Plues, a Steeler fan, remembered the time she and her

Pittsburgh's Franco Harris (32) broke Larry Csonka's Super Bowl mark by rolling up 158 yards, and flattened Minnesota in the process.

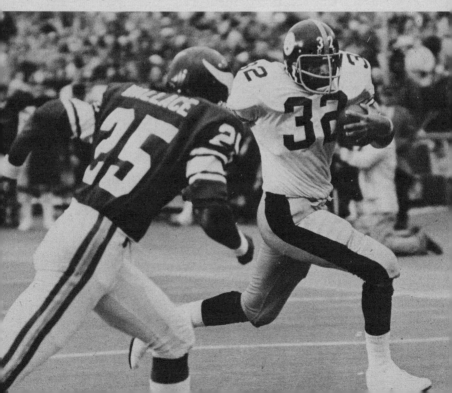

husband waited in line for more than 24 hours in the cold to buy a pair of playoff tickets. Franco, who was leaving the team's offices, came over to visit with them.

There was another time when Harris was riding his bicycle near his Pittsburgh apartment. A young boy spotted him and asked: "Can I ride my bike with you, Franco?"

Soon a dozen boys were riding their bicycles alongside Franco Harris. But the story does not end there. Franco took the boys to his apartment, where he gave them soda and cooked them hot dogs and hamburgers.

So it was easy for the fans to like Franco. He never considered himself special just because he was an athlete. But right now he *was* special. Thanks largely to him, the Steelers were ahead.

The Vikings were an experienced team playing in their third Super Bowl. But they were still looking for their first victory. Fran Tarkenton, their wise and resourceful quarterback, had rescued the Vikings several times during the season, but he could not outsmart the Steeler defense. It was early in the fourth quarter, but already they had intercepted two of his passes and knocked down four more.

Once again, however, a defensive play changed the course of the game. Bobby Walden of the Steelers was in his own end zone ready to punt. But this time Terry Brown rushed through and blocked the kick. The ball rolled loose in the end zone, and Brown fell on it for a touchdown. Dramatically, the Vikings had scored, closing the gap to 9–6. Although the extra-point attempt failed, the game was now very much in doubt.

Could the young Steelers keep their control? Could they score again? Franco Harris was going to do his best. He took a handoff and made eight yards, dragging a couple of Vikings with him. It was third down and two yards to go. Bradshaw realized the Vikings might be looking for Harris once more, so he faked to his fullback and then dropped back to pass. Tight end Larry Brown was open. Bradshaw had one of the strongest arms in football, and he fired a 30-yard pass to Brown. First down on the Vikings' 28. The Steelers and the clock were moving.

Now the Vikings did not know what to expect. Bleier broke loose off the left side and gained 17 yards. Then it was Harris again, gaining four yards and then one yard, before

Viking quarterback Fran Tarkenton is grounded by Pittsburgh linebacker Jack Lambert, to cheers from Steelers L. C. Greenwood (68), Ernie Holmes (63), Joe Greene (75), and Mike Wagner (23).

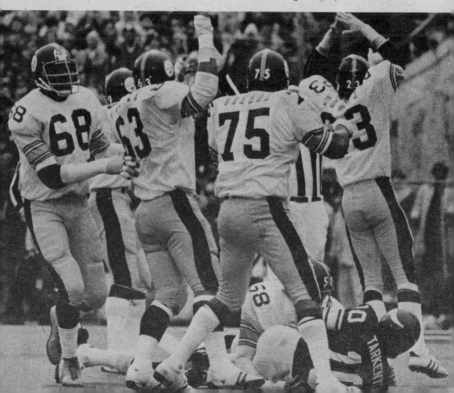

Bradshaw completed a short, six-yard pass to Bleier for a first down on the five-yard line.

After two carries by Harris, Bradshaw sprinted to his right and threw a four-yard touchdown pass to Larry Brown. The Steelers had marched 66 yards like proven veterans. With just three minutes left, they led, 16–6.

Tarkenton was desperate, and the Steelers knew it. His first pass was intercepted by Mike Wagner. As the defense ran happily off the field, Franco Harris came back, ready to run out the clock. There was nothing the Vikings could do. When the gun sounded, the Steelers had won Super Bowl IX, 16–6.

Franco Harris had gained 158 yards—a Super Bowl record—on 34 carries, with one touchdown. Along with the Most Valuable Player award he won a car from *Sport* magazine.

Terry Hanratty, the Steelers' second-string quarterback, remembered driving home once after a game during Harris' rookie season. He passed a familiar-looking hitchhiker. It was Franco Harris. Franco used to take a bus to practice and occasionally hitchhiked home.

Now Mr. MVP had a car of his own.

Super Bowl X

Lynn Swann
The Swann Ballet

When people thought of Lynn Swann, they pictured southern California, where the weather was sunny and warm and the lifestyle was easygoing. They thought of Hollywood and how easily Swann fit into the land of make-believe. And it was true that when Lynn was a youngster, he took tap-dancing lessons and enjoyed being in the spotlight.

But Lynn Swann was born in the small steel mill town of Alcoa, Tennessee, where his father worked at the local airport as a maintenance man. When Lynn was two years old, Willie Swann packed his bags and took his family to San Mateo in northern California. At Serra High School Lynn emerged as an excellent athlete. He was a wide receiver on the football team until his senior year, when he became the quarterback. He was a long-jumper in track and knew how to dunk a basketball even though he was only 5-foot-11.

Colleges began to take notice. Notre Dame was one of the many that offered Lynn a scholarship. But he chose the University of Southern California. Swann became an All-

American wide receiver and was drafted by the Pittsburgh Steelers in 1974. He quickly took his place in the Steeler lineup and became the favorite target of quarterback Terry Bradshaw. As much as anything, it was the combination of Bradshaw to Swann that carried the Steelers to Super Bowl X, their second straight visit to pro football's championship game. The Dallas Cowboys were the opposition this time—on January 18, 1976, in Miami.

Like most wide receivers, he looked like an outcast as he lined up several yards from the rest of the offense, ready to head downfield and duel the defensive backs assigned to stick to him like glue. Lynn Swann took his position opposite Mark Washington of the Cowboys. It was second down with five yards to go, and the Steelers were on the Cowboys' 38.

Quarterback Terry Bradshaw took the snap from center and dropped back to pass. He had one receiver in mind, number 88, Lynn Swann. As he sprinted down the field Swann truly resembled the graceful bird. He gobbled up yardage with his long, loping strides. He was only a wisp of a receiver, 5-foot-11 now and less than 180 pounds, but he had a way of getting open. In a crowd he would outleap opponents as if he were still dunking basketballs in high school.

Bradshaw spotted Swann at the Dallas 16-yard line. Lynn jumped and caught the pass between two defenders for a 32-yard gain and a first down. On the sidelines the Steelers cheered. All their doubts and worries during Super Bowl Week had been erased.

Two weeks earlier, in the American Conference championship game, Swann had been knocked unconscious by

George Atkinson of the Oakland Raiders. He was taken to a hospital where he remained for three days, suffering from a severe concussion. The doctors wanted him to stay even longer, but Swann refused. "The doctors told me I could get dizzy and black out and get sick," Swann remembered. "They said my brain was bruised and it had been bleeding. But if I was afraid of getting hurt, I would quit."

He did not practice until the week before the Super Bowl, and he didn't look good then. "I felt like my head was floating three feet above my body," Swann said. "I just couldn't catch the ball very well. I was worried."

The Steelers were worried too. Swann was an important part of their offense. The Cowboys were not sympathetic. "We're going to intimidate Swann," said Cliff Harris, Dallas' rough and tough defensive back.

Lynn Swann, however, had a lot of courage for a little man playing a big man's game. He had learned not to worry about his size when he was a boy and used to follow his older brother around the San Mateo schoolyards and playgrounds. Calvin Swann always included his brother in choose-up games.

"And I was always the smallest," Lynn said. "I had to learn to play a smarter game."

"The way he gets hit out there, he looks like a baton being twirled around," said Steeler teammate Sam Davis.

"Don't worry, Sam," Swann told Davis. "I don't have time to worry about getting hurt."

Sure enough, Swann had come through for his teammates. His catch gave the Steelers new enthusiasm. The Cowboys had taken an early 7–0 lead, when Roger Staubach threw a 29-yard touchdown pass to Drew Pearson. But now Swann's catch at the Dallas 16 had put the Steelers in a good position to tie the score. Two running plays moved the ball to the seven-yard line. Then Bradshaw rolled out and threw a touchdown pass to Randy Grossman. The score was tied.

Many football people said the Cowboys and the Steelers were the two finest teams in the NFL, and Super Bowl X might be the most memorable of all so far. Each team was looking for its second Super Bowl crown.

After the Steelers scored, Staubach patiently moved the Cowboys 46 yards in 11 plays. When the drive was stalled, Toni Fritsch kicked a 36-yard field goal to put Dallas ahead, 10–7.

The Cowboy defense was not taking any more chances with Swann either. On almost every play he was given double coverage. Bradshaw threw instead to John Stallworth and running backs Franco Harris and Rocky Bleier. But he just could not get the team moving.

Then, just before halftime, Swann broke free. The Cowboys had the Steelers pinned deep in their own territory, so they were not looking for Bradshaw's pass. The play covered 53 yards and gave Pittsburgh a first down on the Cowboys' 37. The Steelers moved to the 19-yard line, where Roy Gerela attempted a 36-yard field goal with 26 seconds remaining in the half. The kick was long enough and high enough—but it was wide to the left. Dallas held on to its 10–7 lead.

No one felt more frustrated than Swann. He had made two big catches, but he felt he wasn't helping the team enough. Lynn, as his mother used to say, loved to be the main attraction, the star performer. As a wide receiver, he sometimes felt that could never happen because a receiver must depend on the quarterback to throw him the ball. "No

Pittsburgh's Lynn Swann makes a diving catch that frustrates Dallas cornerback Mark Washington in Super Bowl X.

matter how good you are," Swann said, "you're always going to be in the quarterback's shadow."

Swann's frustration continued in the third quarter. An interception by J. T. Thomas had given the Steelers the ball on the Cowboys' 25-yard line. Twice Bradshaw threw to Swann, but one pass sailed over his head in the end zone and the other was batted down by the defense. When

Gerela tried another field goal, it too was wide. The Steelers looked depressed, and even a 12-yard completion from Bradshaw to Swann late in the quarter did not lift their spirits.

The Pittsburgh defense was doing its job, however, and early in the fourth quarter the Steelers' special teams came through as well.

Mitch Hoopes of the Cowboys attempted to punt from his own end zone, but the kick was blocked by Reggie Harrison. The ball rolled through the end zone and was ruled a safety. "It was the first punt I ever blocked in my life," a happy Harrison told his teammates on the sidelines.

The Cowboys' lead was cut to 10–9. This seemed to be just what the Steelers needed. On their next possession Bradshaw kept the ball on the ground in the trusty hands of Harris and Bleier and marched the team into field-goal range. This time Gerela was on target, booting a 36-yard field goal. With nine minutes left in the game, the Steelers led for the first time, 12–10.

And before the offense could catch its breath, safety Mike Wagner intercepted a Staubach pass putting the Steelers on the Cowboys' seven-yard line. The Cowboys refused to budge as Harris and Bleier tried to score. Gerela was called on again, and he kicked an 18-yard field goal to give the Steelers a 15–10 lead.

Not many in the crowd of more than 80,000 in the Orange Bowl thought the lead was secure, though. Nor did many of the players. So even though they had the ball with only 4:25 to go, the Steelers were looking for more points. It was third down on their own 36-yard line.

"Listen," Lynn Swann told his teammates in the huddle. "I may not have been doing anything all day but I'm ready now when we need the big play." Swann wanted Bradshaw to throw him the ball. And that is just what the quarterback did. He dropped back and threw a long pass that Swann caught with a leap on the five-yard line. The wide receiver had put to good use all his training as a basketball player and long-jumper—even as a dancer. He landed and spun toward the end zone, running in for the touchdown. The Steelers missed the extra point, but they now had a 21–10 lead with three minutes left.

It was a spectacular play made by someone who had a flair for the dramatic—someone who had gone to college near Hollywood. "I'm a ham," Swann said. "If I could sing, I'd be dangerous."

But these were the Dallas Cowboys, and quarterback Roger Staubach knew something about being a hero too. He moved the Cowboys 80 yards in only five plays, finishing up with a 34-yard touchdown pass to Percy Howard. The Steelers' lead was cut to 21–17.

And when Bradshaw and the offense were unable to run out the clock, the Cowboys got one final chance to win. They took over on their 39-yard line with 1:22 remaining. On first down Staubach scrambled for 11 yards to the 50. Many in the crowd were standing now, waiting for a miracle finish. Staubach dropped back to pass and completed one to Preston Pearson on the Steelers' 38. First down again with less than a minute to play.

Two more passes by Staubach were incomplete. Then, on third down, he spotted Drew Pearson near the Steelers' end zone. But the ball never got to Pearson. Safety Glen Edwards stepped in for the interception, and the victory was saved. The Steelers had won their second Super Bowl in a row, 21–17.

Lynn Swann had returned from a serious injury to give life to the Steelers' offense and to make the biggest catches of the day. He had four receptions for 161 yards and one touchdown. One of the game's biggest little men, Swann was voted the Most Valuable Player, the first receiver to win that honor.

Super Bowl XI

Fred Biletnikoff
An Unlikely Hero

Ephraim Biletnikoff was delighted even though he did not understand how his son Fred could be paid so much money for playing a game. When Ephraim was a young man he was a boxer—and a pretty good one too. He was the Amateur Athletic Union lightweight champion and later fought professionally, although he never earned enough from boxing to make a living. Instead, he settled down and raised a family in Erie, Pennsylvania, working as a welder in a steel mill.

Fred Biletnikoff had been a wide receiver at Florida State University, where he teamed with quarterback Steve Tensi to form one of the best passing combinations in collegiate football. Fred wasn't particularly big or fast, but he had great hands and terrific moves.

In the 1965 Gator Bowl, Fred caught four touchdown passes in Florida State's victory over Oklahoma. And after the game Fred signed a $100,000 contract with the Oakland Raiders while standing under the goalposts in front of a national television audience. The next day, back at Florida

State, Fred signed another contract. He married his college sweetheart under his college goalposts.

Biletnikoff went on to become an outstanding receiver in pro football and was one of the main reasons the Raiders were in Pasadena, California, on January 9, 1977. They were there along with the Minnesota Vikings for Super Bowl XI.

Everyone knew that Fred Biletnikoff was the nervous type. For instance, he was never able to eat on the day of a game, and he usually had only one meal the day before. Fred developed an ulcer when he was in high school, and it always acted up during the football season. Before the start of Super Bowl XI, while the Raiders were waiting to be introduced, Biletnikoff stood in the tunnel under the stands at the Rose Bowl and smoked a cigarette trying to calm down.

Now, when the Raiders had the ball for the second time in the game, Fred thought the best medicine would be to catch a pass. Quarterback Ken Stabler agreed. With a first down on the 31-yard line, Stabler spotted Biletnikoff over the middle and fired a perfect pass to him. Fred reached out with his big hands and they seemed to swallow the ball. The play gained nine yards and Biletnikoff and the Raiders were on their way.

Oakland fans were used to the sight of Biletnikoff catching passes. In 12 years he had caught 536 of them, 69 for touchdowns. "And I bet he's caught half of them standing on his head," Stabler said. "Those were passes I had given up on. I think Fred is the best receiver of all time."

The Vikings were certainly treating Biletnikoff with respect. Near the end of the first quarter the Raiders moved into scoring range, but Fred could not get free for any more receptions. Instead Stabler threw to tight end Dave Casper and relied on running back Clarence Davis. The combination moved the ball to the Minnesota seven-yard line before the drive stalled early in the second quarter. Erroll Mann kicked a 24-yard field goal to give the Raiders a 3–0 lead.

Perhaps now, people thought, both teams would not be so conservative. This was the Vikings' fourth appearance in a Super Bowl and they had yet to win. The Raiders had lost Super Bowl II to the Packers but had been a strong team through the years, always on the verge of winning the championship. But because neither of these teams had won the really big game, they were considered almost like losers.

The Raiders took pleasure in being cast as the bad guys. They were used to it. Owner Al Davis had built a team around draft choices and players no one else wanted. Coach John Madden was a big, heavyset man who was good-natured off the field but paced the sidelines and yelled at the officials during the game. His stomach was as nervous as Biletnikoff's.

Madden was starting to feel better, though, as Stabler moved the Raiders into Viking territory again during the second quarter. A pass to Casper was good for 19 yards and a first down on the 26. Then running back Carl Garrett slashed off tackle for 13 yards and carried twice more for seven. Oakland had a third down and three on the six-yard line.

With the Vikings looking for the run, Stabler sought his favorite receiver. He threw a short pass to Biletnikoff, who made the catch at the one-yard line. On the next play Stabler threw to Casper in the end zone for a touchdown. The Raiders led, 10–0.

As Stabler ran off the field he told Madden, "Don't worry, Coach, there's plenty more where that came from."

Quarterback Fran Tarkenton tried to rally the Vikings, but his passes fell incomplete. Time to punt again. Neal Colzie of the Raiders returned the punt 25 yards to the Vikings' 35.

Stabler went to work on the Minnesota defense, sending Davis and fullback Mark van Eeghen up the middle a total of three times. With a first down on the 18-yard line, Stabler spotted Biletnikoff working his way into the clear again and fired a hard pass toward the end zone. Biletnikoff made a diving catch at the one-yard line for another first down. This time Stabler handed off to Pete Banaszak, and the veteran running back ran over the defense for the score. The Raiders suddenly had a 16–0 lead.

Oakland's Fred Biletnikoff scampers for big yardage against Minnesota after catching a Ken Stabler pass that set up a touchdown.

The Raiders congratulated Biletnikoff for setting up those two touchdowns. Even now, with grass stains on his uniform and the black, gooey stickum on his hands to help him hold on to the ball, Fred did not look very much like a football player. He was 6-foot-1, but he weighed only 180 pounds. He had thin, straggly blond hair and had already lost a lot of it. He also was 33 years old and looked 43.

Now, even though the Raiders were well ahead, Biletnikoff could not relax. At halftime he smoked several more cigarettes while Mickey Mouse and Donald Duck, along with 1,425 members of Los Angeles high-school bands, put on a spectacular halftime show.

In the third quarter the Raiders quickly increased their lead to 19–0 when Mann booted a 40-yard field goal. The Vikings finally came to life as Tarkenton took them to the Raiders' eight-yard line. On first down he rolled out and passed to Sammy White in the end zone for a touchdown. The score was 19–7.

As the fourth quarter began, Tarkenton had his team on the move once more. If the Vikings scored, they would be right back in the game and in position to end those years of frustration. Tarkenton completed a nine-yard pass to Stu Voigt for a first down on the Oakland 44.

The Viking quarterback dropped back again, but this time the Raiders put on a heavy rush. He scrambled, looking for a receiver, and finally threw. But Raider linebacker Willie Hall intercepted and returned the ball to his 46-yard line.

Stabler wanted to take advantage of the situation before the Vikings could recover. On second down he spotted Biletnikoff and threw a pass that Fred caught at the 35. Biletnikoff was in the open and headed for the end zone. But he was nailed from behind at the two-yard line by Bobby Bryant.

The Raiders had a first down, but Biletnikoff was unhappy as he ran off the field for a breather. "I'm sorry I got caught, Coach," he told Madden. "But I can't run away from anybody, even the officials."

Even so, he had once again put the Raiders in position to score. Pete Banaszak did the honors on a two-yard run and the Raiders led, 26–7. When Tarkenton began to throw in desperation, Willie Brown, the veteran cornerback who'd been a member of the Raiders' first Super Bowl team, intercepted a pass and ran 75 yards for a touchdown. With five minutes to play, the Raiders led, 32–7.

Many of the 103,424 fans began to leave. The outcome was no longer in doubt. The Vikings did score again, but the Oakland Raiders were the victors in Super Bowl XI, 32–14.

There were many heroes, but because of his clutch catches, Fred Biletnikoff was voted the game's Most Valuable Player. It was, he said, the first award he had ever won.

Super Bowl XII

Harvey Martin and Randy White
The Harvey and Randy Show

It was not until late in his junior year in high school that Harvey Martin decided to try out for the football team. As big as he was, young Harvey was shy and not very aggressive. His family had moved from the Dallas ghetto to a modest working-class neighborhood. He was still unsure of himself, and his sister often fought his battles for him.

Harvey began to get stronger when he made the football team at South Oak Cliff High. He added muscle to his tall, skinny frame. Soon the colleges began to take notice—but because he had so little experience, Harvey chose a small school, East Texas State. It was the best place to continue his football education.

Randy White's childhood was different. He was the son of a Wilmington, Delaware, butcher who wanted him to become a football player. So even though he was an excellent power-hitting first baseman who was drafted by baseball's Philadelphia Phillies, Randy decided to please his father and pursue a football career. He went to Maryland

and in his senior year was named to the All-America team as a defensive end.

White and Martin became teammates, playing shoulder-to-shoulder on the Dallas Cowboys' defensive line. Randy was the right tackle and Harvey the right end that the Denver Broncos would have to deal with when they faced the Cowboys in Super Bowl XII on January 15, 1978, in New Orleans. It was a special day for another reason too: It was Randy White's twenty-fifth birthday.

Like most professional athletes, football players become identified with the city in which they play. The enthusiastic Bronco fans—celebrating their team's first appearance in the Super Bowl—treated every player as if he were a native of Denver. Cowboy rooters were the same. They thought Randy White and Harvey Martin belonged to Dallas. In Martin's case, though, it was true.

Harvey had always been a Cowboy fan. Quarterback Don Meredith was one of his favorites, and Harvey remembered crying when the Cowboys lost to Green Bay in the NFL championship game. He also knew what it meant to grow up black and poor in Dallas. When the school day ended, he worked in the kitchen of a department store restaurant. "I used to scrub the floors," he said. "The detergent was so strong it ruined the soles of my shoes. But I learned the value of a dollar."

Eventually he transferred from an all-black high school to an integrated one and came in contact with white people for the first time. Blacks and whites had problems in Dallas, but the situation was improving.

And color did not matter when you were a Dallas Cowboy. "I wake up every morning telling myself, 'Harvey Martin, you're lucky and don't ever forget it,'" he said.

Denver's Craig Morton considered himself lucky too. He had played 10 years for the Cowboys before they traded him to the Giants in 1974. He had two poor years in New York trying to make the Giants respectable again. Finally they traded the veteran quarterback to Denver, where in 1977 he had one of his finest seasons. The combination of Morton and the Broncos' "Orange Crush" defense had carried them to the Super Bowl. Now, as the teams faced each other in front of 76,400 fans in the New Orleans Superdome, it was a question of whose luck would run out.

Martin and White took their three-point stance and waited for Morton to call a play. It was third and nine on the Cowboys' 33. A big play was needed to keep the Broncos from scoring on their first possession of the game.

Morton had never been the quickest quarterback in the NFL. Now that he was older and his knees were not as strong, he had slowed down even more. The Dallas front four knew they would have to put pressure on him and not give him time to throw. White did just that as he fought through a block by guard Tom Glassic and tackled Morton for an 11-yard loss. The Broncos' drive had been stopped. White had even pushed them out of field-goal range.

The strategy worked even better the next time Denver had the ball. White and Martin and Ed "Too Tall" Jones chased Morton in the backfield, waving their big hands in his face and making him hurry his passes. On second down from his 29-yard line, Morton rushed a pass and it was intercepted by safety Randy Hughes. The Cowboys had a first down on Denver's 25.

Roger Staubach struck quickly, hitting Billy Joe DuPree with a 13-yard completion. Then he turned his running

Dallas defensive demons Randy White (54)—tackling Denver's Craig Morton (7)—and Harvey Martin (79) sacked the quarterback three times in Super Bowl XII.

backs loose. Robert Newhouse and Tony Dorsett pushed the ball closer to the goal line. On fourth down Dorsett ran from the three-yard line into the end zone for a touchdown. The Cowboys took a 7–0 lead.

But the Dallas defense did not let up. Morton must have thought his former teammates had become his escorts, as Martin, White, and Jones were there every time he turned. Morton was rushing his passes even more now, and this time it was Aaron Kyle who intercepted for Dallas. Kyle returned the ball to the Broncos' 40-yard line.

For a moment it looked as if the Cowboys would add another quick touchdown. Newhouse gained nine yards and then Dorsett picked up 18 more. First down on the eight-yard line.

But the Broncos had a good defense, too, and the "Orange Crush" held Dallas right there. On fourth down Efren Herrera kicked a 35-yard field goal to put the Cowboys ahead, 10–0. As the first quarter ended, Morton was still scrambling in the backfield, desperately looking for a receiver while White and Martin closed in on him.

Harvey Martin was actually having fun, but he remembered a time when football had been a painful experience. How could he ever forget the first day he showed up for practice at South Oak Cliff High School?

"We just gave him some old shoes that were a size and a half too small and an old helmet that didn't quite fit," said Ray Mattingly, the high-school coach. "Harvey put them on anyway and went out and played."

A few days later Harvey finally got up the nerve to ask his coach for new equipment. He had blood on his forehead from the cuts the helmet had made, and his toes were sore because of the shoes. "Coach, I need bigger equipment," Harvey said.

Ray Mattingly was amazed. "If a kid could play so well under those conditions," the coach said, "he must be quite a player."

Roger Staubach was also quite a player. At the start of the second quarter he moved the Cowboys 32 yards into field-goal range. Herrera kicked a 43-yarder to make the score 13–0.

When Morton threw a long pass, trying for a quick touchdown, it fell short and Benny Barnes made Dallas' third interception of the game. Halftime.

During the break the stands buzzed with talk about Randy White's outstanding first-half play. Randy had always been a standout, starting in high school when he was already 6-foot-3 and 220 pounds.

White played on a losing team all three years, but it wasn't his fault. "He was so superior to the rest of our team," said Earl Batten, one of the McKean coaches. "On defense Randy tried to cover the whole field himself. He was a fullback on offense."

Mostly, White was the strong, silent type who just did his job. Harvey Martin was three years older than Randy and a lot more outgoing. Harvey liked to talk. He had his own radio show in Dallas—*The Beautiful Harvey Martin Show.*

As halftime came to an end, it was time for "The Harvey and Randy Show" to get back into gear.

The Cowboys defense could not afford to let up. Early in the third quarter Bronco Jim Turner kicked a 47-yard field goal to make it 13–3, and now Denver had the ball again. On third down and 10, Martin burst into the backfield like a runaway tank and tackled Morton for a nine-yard loss. The Broncos punted again.

Martin's defensive play seemed to inspire the offense. Staubach began another drive. On third down from the Denver 45, he threw a long pass into the end zone. Wide receiver Butch Johnson made a diving catch between two defenders for a touchdown. The Cowboys led, 20–3.

Bronco coach Red Miller benched Morton and put in Norris Weese, a quarterback who did not have a strong arm but was more mobile than Morton and perhaps could avoid the Cowboys' rush. The strategy worked. Weese stayed a step ahead of Martin and White after Rick Upchurch returned a kickoff 67 yards to put his team in scoring range. Just like that, Rob Lytle scored from the one, and the score was 20–10.

If the Cowboys' fans were worried, the team was not. As the game headed into the fourth quarter the Cowboys were convinced the Broncos would not score again. Their confidence came from players like Randy White and Harvey Martin.

And no matter how good people said he was, Randy never seemed to listen. He just tried to improve. He was 6-foot-4 and 250 pounds, and most of it was the muscle he developed through weight lifting. His two favorite hobbies were lifting weights and training dogs on his Pennsylvania farm.

But this was no time to think about hobbies. This game was serious business. When the Broncos tried to run, White and Martin plugged the holes with ease. And now, even when Weese tried to pass, the Cowboys were all over him. On third down and four with 8:50 to play, Weese fumbled when he was hit by Martin. Aaron Kyle recovered for the Cowboys on Denver's 29-yard line.

But if anyone thought the Cowboys would try to run out the clock, they were wrong. On first down Staubach handed the ball to Newhouse, who surprised the Broncos by throwing the option pass. Wide receiver Golden Richards caught it in the end zone for a touchdown, and the Dallas fans went wild. With seven minutes to go, the Cowboys had a 27–10 lead. And that was the final score as Dallas won Super Bowl XII.

The defense had intercepted four passes and recovered four fumbles. As symbols of that defense, Randy White and Harvey Martin shared the Most Valuable Player award. They had combined for seven tackles and three quarterback sacks and had helped make all those interceptions possible.

When the award was announced, White said, "I'm shocked." Martin's biggest thrill came the next day when he rode in the victory parade through the streets of his home-town.

Super Bowl XIII

Terry Bradshaw
Here's to the Hillbilly

By the time he was 30 years old he'd already been the quarterback of Pittsburgh's two Super Bowl championship teams. And now Terry Bradshaw was preparing for his third appearance in the NFL's biggest game.

Still, when Terry daydreamed about the past, his fondest memories were not of winning football games, but of a childhood spent romping around the Louisiana countryside. "They were the happiest days, the greatest time of my life," he said.

Bradshaw grew up just outside of Shreveport, Louisiana. Many of his uncles lived nearby, and on Sundays the Bradshaw clan would gather for a traditional cookout. Terry and his cousins and uncles would play baseball and football and other games. Terry had such a strong sense of family that when it was time to go to college, he chose Louisiana Tech because it was close to home.

Bradshaw had perhaps the strongest arm of any quarterback in the country—college or pro. He was so impressive

*that scouts called him the best prospect since Joe Namath.
Because they had finished with a 1–13 record—the worst in
the NFL—the Pittsburgh Steelers had the first pick in the
1970 draft, and they selected Bradshaw, the blond, 6-foot-3,
215-pounder known as "The Louisiana Rifle."*

*Well, it did take time and Terry did struggle, but he fi-
nally lived up to all those great expectations. Now—against
the Dallas Cowboys in Miami on January 21, 1979—he was
going to try to make the Steelers the first team to win three
Super Bowl championships.*

Even the strong wind blowing across the Orange Bowl
field could not muffle the roar of the crowd. It was only minutes into the first quarter of Super Bowl XIII, but both
teams had already provided plenty of thrills. The Dallas
Cowboys had taken the opening kickoff and marched into
Pittsburgh territory before fumbling the ball away on a
tricky end-around play.

Terry Bradshaw wasted no time in moving the Steelers
into scoring range. They now had a first down on the Cowboys' 28-yard line. He dropped back to pass and spotted
John Stallworth open in the end zone. Bradshaw threw one
of those hard bullet passes he had become famous for and
Stallworth clutched it for a touchdown. The Steelers had
struck quickly for a 7–0 lead.

This was just the kind of beginning Bradshaw had hoped
for. In spite of the fact that Bradshaw had led the Steelers to
victories in Super Bowls IX and X, much of the credit for
those wins had gone to the defense as well as to running
back Franco Harris and wide receiver Lynn Swann.

Bradshaw's critics claimed that he was not very smart.
They thought of him as a country bumpkin, a barefoot boy

trying to make it in a big city. After nine years in the NFL he was still having trouble living down the image.

"I don't think you ever do," Terry said. "It haunts you. There is nothing I can do about it, though. In my early years guys called me a hillbilly and didn't try to understand me. I began feeling sorry for myself. Now, I'm prepared for what people will say."

It was interesting to note that Steelers' coach Chuck Noll allowed Bradshaw to call his own plays during a game while Roger Staubach, the intelligent and experienced quarterback of the Cowboys, was not permitted to do so by coach Tom Landry.

As the first quarter continued to unfold it became obvious that Bradshaw would have to listen to boos as well as cheers. He had one pass intercepted, and then he fumbled when hit by defensive end Harvey Martin. Ed "Too Tall" Jones recovered, and the Cowboys had a first down on the Steelers' 41.

With six seconds left in the quarter, Roger Staubach dropped back to pass on third down and threw 13 yards to Tony Hill at the 26. Hill turned and dashed down the sideline into the end zone as the gun sounded. The Cowboys had tied the score at 7–7.

Years before, when he was a rookie, something like this might have disturbed Terry Bradshaw. "I choked my rookie year," he said. "I felt the pressure so much I couldn't respond to it. I couldn't lift up my arm to throw the football without throwing it into the ground. I was afraid I was going to make a mistake. I was afraid I wasn't going to live up to my reputation."

Now Bradshaw was not going to let a few mistakes shake his confidence. Not even after he fumbled again early in the second quarter and the Cowboys' Mike Hegman scooped up the ball and ran 37 yards for a touchdown. The Cowboys led, 14–7, but Bradshaw did not panic.

The Dallas fans in the crowd of 78,656 stopped cheering when, on the third down and five from his 25, Bradshaw completed a 10-yarder to Stallworth. Defensive back Aaron Kyle missed the tackle, and suddenly Stallworth had an open field. The speedy wide receiver headed for the end zone, taking long, graceful strides that carried him there in no time. The play covered 75 yards and the touchdown tied the score, 14–14.

Quarterbacks live dangerously, but Pittsburgh's Terry Bradshaw (12), who has just lost possession of the ball to Dallas' Mike Hegman, came out on top in the end.

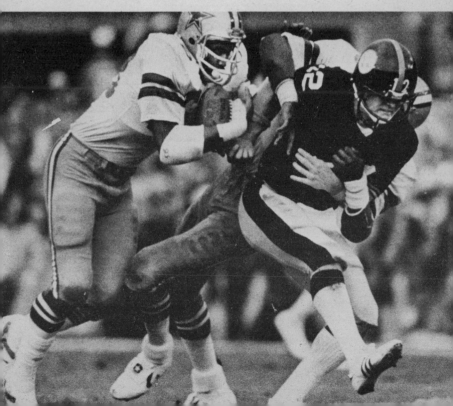

This was one of the few times that a Super Bowl game was as exciting as the fans thought it should be. There was a lot of close action between Steelers who were building a dynasty and Cowboys who were determined to avenge a Super Bowl defeat by Pittsburgh three years earlier. And the second quarter wasn't over.

Late in the period Mel Blount intercepted a pass to put the Steelers in scoring range. Bradshaw completed a pass to Lynn Swann for 29 yards and a first down on the Cowboys' 37. With only 1:30 to play in the half, Bradshaw threw again to Swann, this time for 21 yards. The next pass was incomplete. Then Bradshaw handed off to Franco Harris on a draw play, and Harris gained nine yards. It was third and one at the seven-yard line. There were just 33 seconds remaining. The Steelers were racing the clock.

The Cowboys lined up expecting the Steelers to run for a first down. Instead, Bradshaw rolled to his right and spotted running back Rocky Bleier in the end zone. He threw a soft looping pass that floated into Bleier's arms like a balloon. Touchdown. The last-minute drive had given the Steelers a 21–14 halftime lead.

Bradshaw smiled as he trotted to the locker room. The cheers of the crowd were carrying him as if he were riding on a cloud. He had to admit he liked being a hero. He remembered that when he was in high school he'd even liked getting minor injuries because it brought him a lot of attention.

"I loved it," he said. "I loved getting scratches and cuts and sprained fingers—anything that would show I played football. I wrapped them up real big and at school all the girls would say, 'Oh, you poor baby.' It was great."

Yes, this country boy was really a ham. Bradshaw liked to play pranks on his teammates, and he loved to sing country

& western songs. But as for all that athletic ability, he said he got it from his mother. "She's an excellent athlete," Terry said. "Basketball, Ping-Pong, bowling—she's tough. And very competitive."

Her son would have to be competitive, too, if the Steelers were going to stay on top in Super Bowl XIII. The Cowboys weren't ready to give up yet. In the third quarter Staubach guided the Cowboys into field-goal range, and Rafael Septien kicked a 27-yarder to narrow the deficit to 21–17. Things were looking brighter for Dallas.

Later in the period the Steelers took over on their own 15-yard line. Bradshaw had a long way to go. He completed a pass to Randy Grossman for nine yards and another to Swann for 13. Then, on the second down from his own 44, Bradshaw threw a long pass intended for Swann, who was sprinting down the right sideline. The pass fell incomplete, but an official dropped a yellow flag. Cowboy cornerback Benny Barnes was penalized for tripping Swann. The Steelers had a first down on the Dallas 23.

The Cowboys were angry, but it did them no good. On third and nine from the 22, Bradshaw had a surprise for them. Instead of passing, he handed off to Harris, and the big fullback burst through the line and chugged 22 yards into the end zone. The touchdown gave the Steelers a 28–17 lead.

The Steelers' fans were overjoyed. They waved yellow towels with black lettering that said "Terrible Towel." And they waved their towels even harder when Randy White, the defensive tackle playing on the kicking team, fumbled the kickoff. Roy Winston recovered for the Steelers. First down on the 18-yard line.

Only seven minutes remained. Bradshaw dropped back to

pass, and there was Swann all alone in the back of the end zone. The toss was perfect, and Swann cradled the ball like a baby for another touchdown. The Steelers moved out to a 35–17 advantage.

Roger Staubach, however, was not about to offer his congratulations yet. Many fans hardly noticed as he moved the Cowboys into scoring range, throwing picture passes to Drew Pearson and Billy Joe DuPree and giving the ball to Tony Dorsett, who chewed off big yardage against a relaxed Steeler defense. With just 2:27 to go in the game, Staubach tossed a seven-yard scoring pass to DuPree to make it 35–24.

Everyone took notice when Dennis Thurman recovered an onside kick to give the Cowboys the ball on their 48-yard line. Coolly and calmly, Staubach went to work again, relying solely on the pass now to move his team. With 26 seconds remaining and the ball on the four-yard line, Staubach threw a touchdown pass to Butch Johnson. The score was 35–31, and everyone in the Orange Bowl was stunned.

Could Dallas do it again? Could the Cowboys recover another onside kick? Rafael Septien tried. The ball rolled free for 10 yards with 22 players chasing it. But it was Rocky Bleier who fell on it, giving the Steelers possession. Bradshaw ran out the clock, and Pittsburgh won Super Bowl XIII, 35–31.

This time it was Bradshaw's turn to accept the award as the Most Valuable Player. He'd completed 17 of 30 passes for 318 yards and four touchdowns. His yardage and touchdowns were Super Bowl records. Maybe now people would admit he was more than a simple hillbilly.

Terry Bradshaw
The Ballad of a Steeler

Even during a winning season Terry Bradshaw looked forward to the last game. As soon as it was over, he would pack up and head for his 400-acre ranch near Shreveport, Louisiana, only 30 miles from his boyhood home. It is named the Circle-12 because that is the number Bradshaw wears.

During the off-season Terry would relax in his swimming pool to soothe the aches and pains that came from being a quarterback in the NFL. But the Pittsburgh Steeler superstar worked hard on the ranch, too, cleaning out the stalls and keeping things in order.

It was no different on January 20, 1980. Terry would soon be on his ranch again. But first there was another Super Bowl to play. The Steelers, winners of three Super Bowls in as many attempts were trying for number 4 against the Los Angeles Rams in Pasadena, California.

He was a celebrity now. He was the toast of Pittsburgh, a city of hard-working people who hadn't taken to this country boy at first. He was a country & western singer who had recorded his first album. And there was talk of his going to Hollywood to make movies or star in a television series.

Still, success really hadn't changed Terry Bradshaw. He was a private person who spent many evenings alone in his apartment overlooking Three Rivers Stadium in Pittsburgh. Terry and his wife, Olympic figure skater JoJo Starbuck, were very religious, and Bradshaw liked to read the Bible for inspiration.

On the field Bradshaw was an experienced and knowledgeable quarterback who was now considered the best in the game. "When Terry matured, we matured too," teammate Franco Harris said.

So it was no surprise that the Steelers were big favorites to defeat the Rams in Super Bowl XIV. Coached by Ray Malavasi, Los Angeles had finished the regular season with an unimpressive 9-7 record, but then played like champions during the playoffs. Malavasi and his young quarterback, Vince Ferragamo, were going to have to be lucky and good to beat the powerful Steelers. That became apparent early in the game when Bradshaw moved his team into field-goal range with a 32-yard pass to Harris. Matt Bahr kicked a 41-yarder to give the Steelers a quick 3–0 lead, and the crowd of 103,985 at Pasadena's Rose Bowl began to wonder whether this was going to be a one-sided contest.

Ferragamo had other plans, though. On the Rams' next possession, he completed a six-yard pass to Wendell Tyler to move the ball to his own 47. Then Tyler, the hard-to-catch running back from nearby UCLA, went around left end and broke into the open for a 39-yard gain. The Rams had a first down on the Steelers' 14. And five plays later they had a touchdown when Cullen Bryant scored from one yard out. Los Angeles led, 7–3.

Young Ferragamo, 25, had done well. And Terry Bradshaw, 31, enjoyed the challenge. He remembered his early days in the NFL. He hadn't been brash and confident like Vince. And he hadn't been too happy to find himself drafted by the Steelers. He had barely heard of Pittsburgh. It could have been on Mars. If he was going to play pro

The Steelers' Terry Bradshaw pitches out to Franco Harris (32) for the start of a run that gave Pittsburgh the lead over Los Angeles in the second quarter.

football, he wanted it to be in Dallas or Houston or New Orleans—teams in the South where he was comfortable.

"Being a home boy and a momma's boy, I would have rather stayed close to home," he explained.

Over the years Bradshaw had found a home away from home with the Steelers. And now, even though his team was down, 7–3, he kept his confidence.

Late in the first quarter, Terry had his team on the move again, mixing running and passing plays so well that the Rams seemed confused. A 12-yard pass to Lynn Swann gave the Steelers a first down on the Rams' 18-yard line as the quarter ended.

When play continued, Bradshaw fired a 13-yard completion to Bennie Cunningham. First down on the five. On third down, with the ball on the one and the Rams expecting a run up the middle, Bradshaw pitched out to Harris, who circled right end for a score. The Steelers had regained the lead, 10–7.

Ferragamo and Wendell Tyler were playing inspired football, though. It looked as if they were in their fourth Super Bowl instead of their first. Tyler hammered away at the Steelers' defensive line, gaining five and six yards a carry. Ferragamo threw short safe passes to his backs, Tyler and Lawrence McCutcheon, who then turned those plays into big gains. The Rams quickly reached field-goal range, and Frank Corral kicked a 31-yarder to tie the score at 10–10.

Now Bradshaw was worried. He wanted to give the Steelers the lead again before halftime, but he had only three minutes to do it. So Terry dropped back and threw a pass intended for Sidney Thornton. It never got to him. Dave Elmendorf, the strong safety, stepped in front of Thornton and intercepted.

As the final minutes of the half ticked away, Ferragamo completed three passes, moving the ball to the Steelers' 13. When the drive stalled and Ferragamo was tackled for a 14-yard loss, Frank Corral came back onto the field to try another field goal. This one, from 45 yards, was good too. At halftime the surprising Rams held a 13–10 lead.

In the locker room Terry Bradshaw talked to his teammates. "Ferragamo is doing some job. Every time we score, he comes right back. I told you guys this wasn't going to be an easy game. No one believed me."

The fired-up Steelers struck quickly in the third quarter. Larry Anderson returned the kickoff to his own 39-yard line, giving Bradshaw excellent field position. After Rocky Bleier and Franco Harris carried the ball three times for a first down, Terry threw a 47-yard touchdown pass to Swann. The Steelers were back in front, 17–13.

But it seemed as if Ferragamo was trying to imitate Bradshaw. The young quarterback had a strong arm, too, and he knew how to use it. On the Rams' next possession, he threw a 50-yard strike to Billy Waddy to give Los Angeles a first down on the Steelers' 24. The Steelers' "Iron Curtain" defense looked more like tinfoil.

On the next play the Rams embarrassed the Steelers even more. Ferragamo handed off to McCutcheon, who began to run around right end. But then he stopped and raised his right arm to throw. He spotted Ron Smith alone in the end zone and completed a 24-yard option pass for a touchdown. As the third quarter ended, the Rams led, 19–17.

Terry Bradshaw had been under pressure before. The last time he could remember feeling this kind of pressure was a few years earlier when he sang at a country & western music festival. "I was so nervous my throat was frozen," he said. "I quit after four songs." And he'd felt even worse when he recorded his first album.

But in the huddle he was calm and clearly in charge. A messenger brought in a play from the bench. "Okay, John," Terry said to wide receiver John Stallworth. "This play is for you. Sixty-prevent and go."

The Steelers came to the line of scrimmage with a third down and eight from their 27-yard line. Bradshaw dropped back to pass, and Stallworth ran the special play. Now he was in the open, racing past the defensive backs. Bradshaw threw the ball, and Stallworth caught it at the 32-yard line. He raced the rest of the way for a touchdown. In dramatic style the Steelers had regained the lead, 24–19.

Bradshaw congratulated Stallworth as they trotted to the sidelines. "Imagine that," Bradshaw said. "We tried that play eight times in practice and it never worked."

It was too early to celebrate, however. The pesky Rams would not quit. Ferragamo began another drive with a 24-yard completion to Preston Dennard, and soon they had a first down on the Pittsburgh 32. Ferragamo looked to pass once more and thought he saw Ron Smith open. But this time the Steelers' defense came up with the big play. Linebacker Jack Lambert intercepted the pass and returned it 16 yards.

With 5:24 left to play, the fans expected Bradshaw to run out the clock. Terry, however, knew the slim five-point lead was not safe. On the third down from his 33-yard line, he completed a 45-yard pass to Stallworth. It was first down on the Rams' 22. He passed again, and defensive back Pat Thomas was called for interference in the end zone. With two minutes to play, the Steelers had a first down on the one-yard line.

John Stallworth races untouched for the deciding Pittsburgh touchdown on a Terry Bradshaw pass.

The Ram defense pushed back two thrusts by Franco Harris. But on the third attempt Harris barged into the end zone for the touchdown. The Steelers led, 31–19, and now Bradshaw could relax. The clock ran out on the Rams—and the Steelers had won their fourth Super Bowl in as many tries.

Bradshaw had completed 14 out of 21 passes for 309 yards and two touchdowns. For the second year in a row he was named the Most Valuable Player.

Jim Plunkett
Up from the Barrio

It was called the Barrio, the Spanish-speaking neighborhood in San Jose, California. The people were poor and it felt like Christmas whenever anybody got a new pair of shoes or jeans. Willie and Carmen Plunkett had three children—two girls and a boy named Jim. Life in the Barrio was even tougher for the Plunketts than it was for their neighbors: Mrs. Plunkett was totally blind and her husband was legally blind, which meant he could barely see his hand when he held it in front of his face.

So at an age when most children are being waited on by their parents, Jim Plunkett and his sisters were cooking meals for their family and working odd jobs after school to help pay the bills. Jim Plunkett did not have much, but he had a strong right arm. His parents insisted he stay in school, and he soon earned a scholarship to Stanford University. People were already saying he was a good enough quarterback to play in the NFL.

Plunkett did not disappoint those people. He won the

Heisman Trophy as the best collegian in America in his senior year and led Stanford to a Rose Bowl victory against Ohio State. Early the following spring he was the number 1 draft choice of the New England Patriots of the NFL. Jim's only regret was that his father had died during his sophomore year and never saw him become a star.

Plunkett's professional career had its ups and downs. But on January 25, 1981, it was at its peak. He had brought the Oakland Raiders to Super Bowl XV, where they would play the Philadelphia Eagles in the New Orleans Superdome.

Jim Plunkett knew it would be this way. Everywhere he went during Super Bowl Week, the lights, cameras, and reporters would be close behind. Jim had had a taste of media attention in 1970 when he'd won the Heisman Trophy and been in the Rose Bowl game. Still, he was a quiet man who did not like publicity.

He talked to the reporters and answered all their questions. But his mind kept wandering back to his childhood and the wonderful talks he'd had with his father. He loved those.

Willie Plunkett would get up at 4 a.m. every morning. Even though he could barely see, he sold newspapers at a local post office in San Jose. As Willie prepared breakfast Jim would sit opposite his father at the table, doing his homework. "How is school, Jimmy?" Mr. Plunkett would ask. "How are you doing in sports?" Young Jim would tell his father everything in an excited voice. Now he imagined his father saying, "How's the Super Bowl, Jimmy?"

Carmen Plunkett was 68 years old and not well enough to travel to New Orleans, but every day Jim called her after practice. She always gave him some advice.

"Hold on to the ball, Jimmy," she told him. "Son, they're going to try and take it away from you."

And Jim Plunkett would laugh. Imagine that. After all these years his mother had become a football expert.

It was quite a relief for Plunkett when Sunday came and the Oakland Raiders and the Philadelphia Eagles took the field at the Superdome. No one would be able to interview him during the game.

Actually, Raider owner Al Davis had received most of the attention during Super Bowl Week. He wanted to move his team to Los Angeles, where there was a bigger stadium and more profits than in Oakland, but NFL commissioner Pete Rozelle and the rest of the owners opposed him. Davis had taken the league to court.

The Raiders had always been considered the outcasts in the league, a team of players no one else wanted. Jim Plunkett fit the image. After playing five years in New England, he'd asked to be traded to San Francisco, which was near his hometown. But after two bad years he was released. The Raiders signed him in 1978, and Plunkett sat on the bench for two seasons.

Jim had thought about quitting, but fortunately he decided to give it one more try. When quarterback Dan Pastorini broke his leg in the fifth game of the 1980 season, Plunkett came off the bench to lead the Raiders to 12 victories in 14 games and their third Super Bowl appearance. "I'm the same quarterback I've always been," he said. "It's timing. You have to be lucky enough to be on the right team at the right time."

Now he could feel the excitement, and his hands trembled a little when the Raiders got the ball for the first time. What a great opportunity. Linebacker Rod Martin had intercepted a pass thrown by Ron Jaworski to give the Raiders a first down on the Eagles' 30-yard line.

Plunkett stayed on the ground, giving the ball to Mark van Eeghen and Kenny King. Oakland moved to the 19. Then Plunkett dropped back to pass and completed one to Cliff Branch on the five. First down.

Van Eeghen carried twice, trying to force his way across the goal line. But on the third down from the two, Plunkett faked and threw into the end zone to Branch. Touchdown. The Raiders led, 7–0.

There was only 1:06 remaining in the first quarter when the Raiders got the ball for the third time. They were on their own 14-yard line, and it seemed like good strategy to play it safe from here. Plunkett handed off to King for two yards, then completed a short pass to Branch for four more. It was third and four from the 20, and Plunkett wanted to throw short again. "Just go down about six yards, Kenny," he told King in the huddle. "All we want is the first down."

But the Eagles' rush forced Plunkett to change his plans. He scrambled in the backfield, desperately looking for a receiver. Jim wasn't much of a runner. He had bad knees and a bad left shoulder and his weight had climbed from 210 pounds to 230. Besides, he had a painful groin injury. With every step he took, he felt as if he was being stabbed with a knife.

Still, he got away long enough to spot King, who had broken free at the 39-yard line. Plunkett's pass was perfect, and the quick running back did the rest. King ran down the sideline all the way for a touchdown. The play covered 80 yards and left the Eagles dazed. The Raiders led, 14–0.

Plunkett and King embraced on the sidelines. Their teammates were cheering, and even first-year coach Tom

Flores was smiling. Flores had been the Raiders' first quarterback in their old American Football League days. Now he was watching another Raider quarterback write one of the most thrilling comeback stories in football history.

Plunkett, of course, thought the press was making too big a deal about his season. Sure, he had known bad times as a pro quarterback. He had undergone seven major operations since high school. But all Jim kept saying was that football wasn't nearly as tough as his early life had been.

When he was only in third grade, he got a job cleaning a gas station after school. When he was older, he delivered newspapers until someone stole his bicycle. He worked in a grocery store and in the fields, picking cherries and apricots for 17 cents a bucket. The pay scale was somewhat higher in the Super Bowl—each winning player would receive $18,000, each loser $9,000—and, besides, what fun Plunkett and his teammates were having.

By halftime the Raiders were leading, 14–3. The Eagles had been able to score only on Tony Franklin's 30-yard field goal in the second quarter.

The Raiders took the second-half kickoff and found themselves on their 14-yard line again. Van Eeghen gained eight yards, and Plunkett completed a 13-yard pass to King to give them some breathing room. Then he found a new target. With plenty of time to pass, Plunkett completed a 32-yarder to Bob Chandler. First down on the Eagles' 33.

The Oakland offensive line, led by veterans Gene Upshaw and Art Shell, knew their quarterback could not run, so they worked extra hard to protect him. So after van Eeghen gained four yards to the 29, there was Plunkett in the backfield, taking his time, looking for a receiver. He found one in Cliff Branch, who broke into the clear near the goal line.

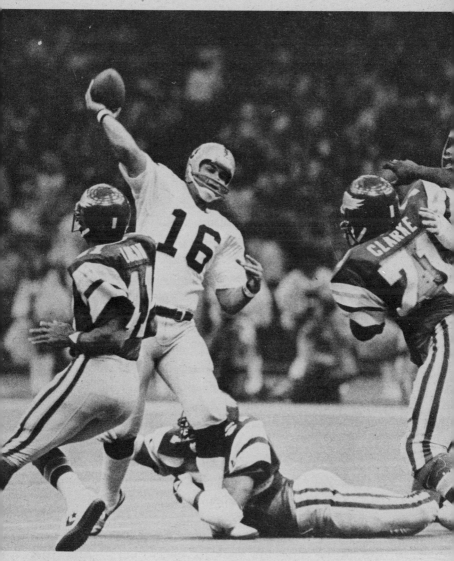

Oakland's Jim Plunkett capped his comeback with a storybook performance against Philadelphia in Super Bowl XV.

Once more Plunkett's pass was perfect. Branch caught it at the one-yard line and stepped into the end zone for the score. The Raiders had increased their lead to 21–3.

This team of outcasts was making life difficult for the Eagles. Quarterback Ron Jaworski knew he had to throw, and the Raiders knew it too. Rod Martin intercepted his second pass, and with 8:20 to go in the third quarter, Oakland had a first down on its 32. If the 75,500 fans at the Superdome expected Plunkett to play it safe, they were wrong. He completed a 16-yarder to tight end Raymond Chester and a 17-yarder to Chandler. Finally, at the Eagles' 28, the defense stiffened and the Raiders were forced to try a field goal. As Plunkett watched from the sidelines, Chris Bahr booted a 46-yarder to make the score 24–3.

Every part of Jim Plunkett's body ached, but he did not mind. Only one more quarter to play and he would have the biggest victory of his career—a career that had been written off many times. When he was in high school, the doctors had found lumps in his neck. They thought he might have cancer. Fortunately for Plunkett, the lumps on his neck were not cancerous. "I learned there were more important things in life than football," he said.

Even so, football was what was important to Plunkett on this January day. Although the Eagles finally scored a touchdown on Jaworski's eight-yard pass to Keith Krepfle, nothing was going to spoil this day for Jim and the Raiders. Plunkett came right back, throwing passes to his wide receivers, and Oakland moved into field-goal range. Bahr kicked a 35-yarder and the Raiders led, 27–10.

And that's the way the game ended. Jim Plunkett, the unwanted quarterback, and Al Davis, the owner who had challenged Pete Rozelle, had helped give the Raiders their second Super Bowl victory. In the locker room the players snapped photographs and laughed as Rozelle presented the Vince Lombardi Trophy to Davis.

Reporters surrounded Plunkett, who had been named the game's Most Valuable Player. He had completed 13 out of 21 passes for 261 yards, including three touchdowns. But Plunkett stood there quietly, looking as if he had played for the losing team. He didn't even smile.

"I'm not very good at showing how I feel," he said apologetically. "But I am happy. Believe me, I am."

Joe Montana
The Heart of San Francisco

As a youngster, Joe Montana had spent countless hours in his backyard throwing a football through an old tire. As unexciting as that may seem, it improved the boy's accuracy, and one day it would pay off.

He lived in the mining town of Monongahela, Pennsylvania, and he became a high-school star in football, baseball, and basketball.

Montana's play at quarterback earned him a scholarship to Notre Dame, where he led the Fighting Irish to the national championship in 1977, his junior year, and to a Cotton Bowl triumph the following year against Houston.

In spite of those accomplishments he wasn't drafted by the pros until the third round—by the San Francisco 49ers. As a rookie in 1979, he got a chance to throw the ball only 23 times. But midway through the 1980 season the 6-foot-2, 200-pounder became the starting quarterback. And the next season he guided the 49ers to the promised land—the Sil-

verdome in Pontiac, Michigan, where on January 24, 1982, San Francisco met the Cincinnati Bengals in Super Bowl XVI.

The Silverdome audience of 81,270, plus an estimated 100,000,000 watching on television, were promised a wide-open game by both teams. This was an unusual Super Bowl, not only because the two teams were making their first appearance in the game but also because it was the first time the Super Bowl was being played in the North.

The likelihood of severe winter weather was the reason the NFL had always played its biggest game in the South or on the West Coast. But it could not rain or snow inside the Silverdome.

Detroit, which was the host city even though the game was being played 20 miles away in Pontiac, made all the visitors welcome. It renamed one of its main streets Bourbon Street North (New Orleans, site of several Super Bowls, has its famous Bourbon Street). It offered bus tours of the city and held snowmobile races. There were plenty of buses available to take people to the game. Officials hoped that many fans would leave their cars home and avoid traffic jams.

During Super Bowl Week temperatures hovered around zero, there was snow, and the roads were icy. And on the day of the game, in spite of the buses, there was a huge traffic jam. Even the 49ers were caught in it.

Joe Montana buckled his chin strap and was ready to take the field with the rest of the 49ers' offense. He had just gotten last-minute instructions from Bill Walsh, the silver-haired coach who had transformed the 49ers from the worst team in the NFL into National Conference champions in just three years, and was now eager to work some of his magic on the Bengals.

Walsh was not a typical football coach. He rarely screamed or threatened his players. He wanted them to enjoy being in the Super Bowl. When the team arrived at their hotel in Detroit, Walsh—who had come a few days earlier—dressed up as a doorman and helped carry the players' bags. During practices inside the Silverdome the 49ers listened to rock music so they would get accustomed to the noise.

Walsh was known as an offensive genius who had spent most of his career as an assistant. His specialty was developing quarterbacks, and not only had he helped Montana become one of the best, but he had also taught Bengals' quarterback Ken Anderson. Walsh was proud of his two students and it made this game even more special to him.

But suddenly, without warning, the 49ers were in trouble on the first play of the game. Amos Lawrence fumbled the kickoff, and the Bengals recovered on the 26-yard line. Joe Montana unbuckled his chin strap and watched helplessly as Anderson ran onto the field.

In no time, it seemed, the Bengals were threatening to score. Anderson completed a pass to Isaac Curtis and another to Dan Ross, bringing the Bengals to the five-yard line. Charles Alexander ran up the middle but was stopped for no gain. Anderson then tried to pass but was tackled for a six-yard loss by Jim Stuckey. The 49ers' defense was starting to recover from the shock.

On third down from the 11, Anderson again dropped back to pass. He threw over the middle for Ross, his trusty tight end, but this time defensive back Dwight Hicks stepped in front and intercepted the pass. Before he was tackled, he had carried the ball to the 32-yard line. Now it was time for Joe Montana.

Quickly he took advantage of the interception and began to move the 49ers downfield. Montana was exciting to watch. He liked to roll out and throw on the run. He specialized in scrambling when it looked as if he would be caught. The 49ers had made it to the Super Bowl because he was able to avoid a big rush by the Dallas Cowboys and throw a touchdown pass to Dwight Clark in the final seconds of the NFC title game.

He was giving the Bengals a taste of the same medicine. Montana threw a six-yard pass to running back Ricky Patton, then another six-yarder to Dwight Clark and an eight-yard pass to Freddie Solomon. He liked to use all of his receivers—and sure enough, his fourth pass was to tight end Charle Young who gained 15 yards. The 49ers had a first down on the Bengals' 33.

Montana now turned to the ground game. Earl Cooper broke clear for 10 yards and Bill Ring added seven more. After Cooper was held to a one-yard gain, Montana threw a 14-yard completion to Solomon. First down on the one. This time Joe did the honors himself. He dove over for the touchdown. The 49ers led, 7–0.

The Bengals looked nervous. And even when they made a big play, it was followed by a mistake. Cris Collinsworth fumbled after catching a pass from Anderson at the 49ers' eight-yard line, and Lynn Thomas recovered for San Francisco.

Two running plays gained only three yards, and Montana decided he was not going to play it safe any longer, even

San Francisco's Joe Montana vaults over the Cincinnati line for the game's first touchdown.

when deep in his own territory. It was just not the 49ers' style. On third down he rolled out, avoided a tackler, and completed a 21-yard pass to Solomon. First down on the 32.

Then Montana scrambled for a seven-yard gain and handed off to Cooper for 13 more. The Bengals' defense did not know what to expect next. But Montana knew exactly what he was doing.

He was only 25 years old, the second youngest quarterback to play in the Super Bowl, and yet he showed remarkable self-confidence. Joe Namath had been only a day older when he led the Jets to victory in Super Bowl III.

Montana did not have Namath's arm or swinging lifestyle, but he had the same ability to take charge in the huddle. John Brodie, a former 49er quarterback, noticed this when Montana was just a rookie. "I can't define it," Brodie said, "but Joe knows what he's doing. Joe Montana, I think, will become the best quarterback who ever played the game."

After starting at the eight, Montana had guided the 49ers to the Bengals' 11-yard line. On first down he looked to pass and spotted Cooper open over the middle. He threw the ball perfectly, and the big fullback rumbled into the end zone for a touchdown. The 49ers had a 14–0 lead.

Montana clapped his hands and was one of the first to congratulate Cooper. "I am affected by things," he said, "but I usually don't show it."

Soon there would be more celebrating. He took the 49ers on another long drive that resulted in a 22-yard field goal by Ray Wersching with 15 seconds remaining in the first half. Then, on the kickoff, Wersching booted the ball low and it bounced crazily on the Astroturf. One Bengal, then another, and still another were unable to hold on to the ball. Milt

McColl of the 49ers recovered at the Cincinnati four-yard line, and with only two seconds left, Wersching kicked a 26-yard field goal. At halftime the amazing 49ers led, 20–0.

At Notre Dame, Montana had become famous as the "Comeback Kid," coming off the bench to lead his team to victory. His most memorable game was the Cotton Bowl in 1978. Houston had taken a 34–12 lead in the fourth quarter, but Montana had rallied the Irish and, with four seconds to play, threw the touchdown pass that gave them a 35–34 victory. That was when Bill Walsh knew he had the qualities to be a great professional quarterback. "Early in Joe's second year I knew he would be our quarterback," the coach said. "We just eased him in carefully."

But Ken Anderson also knew how to come from behind, and the Bengals had made their own reputation for being a comeback team. Early in the third quarter Anderson ran five yards for a touchdown to cut the lead to 20–7.

Minutes later the Bengals were threatening again with a first down on the three-yard line. Four times they tried to score and four times they were turned back by the proud 49ers defense. On fourth down fullback Pete Johnson was stopped inches from the goalline.

It was a magnificent stand but the 49ers were left with poor field position. Montana did not take any chances, and soon San Francisco punted.

Back came Anderson, not at all discouraged by the 49ers' defense. He took the Bengals 54 yards to a touchdown, tossing a four-yard pass to Dan Ross for the score. Now it was 20–14. And the Bengals' fans were going wild. Some were dressed in orange and black tiger stripes and some had painted their faces the same colors. But this was the type of situation that brought out the best in Joe Montana. He loved the challenge.

"I remember when he was ten years old and he wanted to quit midget football," noted his father, Joe, Sr. "I said: 'Get your equipment; you're going to practice. One day, Joey, things are going to get tough in your life and you're going to want to quit. I don't believe in that.' "

With the Bengals playing inspired football, Montana dug into his bag of tricks and pulled out a 17-yard completion to Mike Wilson to begin another drive. He stayed mostly on the ground this time, calmly moving the 49ers into field-goal range. Wersching connected from 40 yards away, and it was 23–14. The 49ers had some breathing room.

Time was slipping away for the Bengals. Only 5:45 remained and Anderson was forced to pass. Eric Wright intercepted. San Francisco had a first down on the 22-yard line.

Montana took no chances, handing off to his running backs and, on one play, scrambling himself for six yards. On fourth down with 1:57 to go, Wersching kicked his fourth field goal, this time from 23 yards away, and the 49ers' lead was 26–14.

And still Anderson tried. He threw six passes and completed them all, the last traveling three yards to Dan Ross, who was in the end zone. With 16 seconds showing on the clock, the score was 26–21. But when the Bengals attempted an onside kick, Dwight Clark recovered and the 49ers held on to win their first championship.

In the locker room coach Walsh received a congratulatory telephone call from President Ronald Reagan. And Joe Montana, who had completed 14 out of 22 passes for 157 yards and a touchdown, was voted the Most Valuable Player.

It's a joyous time in the dressing room for Joe Montana as he grips his Most Valuable Player trophy.

Before the game, when the 49er team bus was stalled in traffic, Montana had played a tape that captured the spirit of Super Sunday. It's called "This Is It." For Montana and San Francisco, this was it.

Super Bowl Box Scores

Following is a scoring summary for each Super Bowl. The top portion of the summary is a period-by-period listing of the points scored by each team, with totals in the last column. Below that is a listing of every play in which points were made. For example, "**GB**—McGee 37 pass from Starr (Chandler kick)" means that Green Bay's Max McGee scored a touchdown on a 37-yard pass from Bart Starr, and Don Chandler added the extra point. Later in the game, "**KC**—FG Mercer 31" means that Kansas City's Mike Mercer kicked a 31-yard field goal. Scoring is listed in the order that it occurred. The last reference in each box score, "Att," means attendance.

Super Bowl I at Los Angeles
January 15, 1967

Kansas City (AFL)	0	10	0	0—10
Green Bay (NFL)	7	7	14	7—35

GB—McGee 37 pass from Starr (Chandler kick); KC—McClinton 7 pass from Dawson (Mercer kick); GB—Taylor 14 run (Chandler kick); KC—FG Mercer 31; GB—Pitts 5 run (Chandler kick); GB—McGee 13 pass from Starr (Chandler kick); GB—Pitts 1 run (Chandler kick). Att—61,946.

Super Bowl II at Miami
January 14, 1968

Green Bay (NFL)	3	13	10	7—33
Oakland (AFL)	0	7	0	7—14

GB—FG Chandler 39; GB—FG Chandler 20; GB—Dowler 62 pass from Starr (Chandler kick); OAK—Miller 23 pass from Lamonica (Blanda kick); GB—FG Chandler 43; GB—Anderson 2 run (Chandler kick); GB—FG Chandler 31; GB—Adderley 60 interception return (Chandler kick); OAK—Miller 23 pass from Lamonica (Blanda kick). Att—75,546.

Super Bowl III at Miami
January 12, 1969

New York Jets (AFL)   0   7   6   3—16
Baltimore (NFL)   0   0   0   7— 7

NY—Snell 4 run (Turner kick); NY—FG Turner 32; NY—FG Turner 30; NY—FG Turner 9; BAL—Hill 1 run (Michaels kick). Att—75,389.

Super Bowl IV at New Orleans
January 11, 1970

Minnesota (NFL)   0   0   7   0— 7
Kansas City (AFL)   3   13   7   0—23

KC—FG Stenerud 48; KC—FG Stenerud 32; KC—FG Stenerud 25; KC—Garrett 5 run (Stenerud kick); MIN—Osborn 4 run (Cox kick); KC—Taylor 46 pass from Dawson (Stenerud kick). Att—80,562.

Super Bowl V at Miami

January 17, 1971

Baltimore (AFC)	0	6	0	10—16
Dallas (NFC)	3	10	0	0—13

DALL—FG Clark 14; **DALL**—FG Clark 30; **BAL**—Mackey 75 pass from Unitas (kick blocked); **DALL**—Thomas 7 pass from Morton (Clark kick); **BAL**—Nowatzke 2 run (O'Brien kick); **BAL**—FG O'Brien 32. Att—79,204.

Super Bowl VI at New Orleans

January 16, 1972

Dallas (NFC)	3	7	7	7—24
Miami (AFC)	0	3	0	0— 3

DALL—FG Clark 9; **DALL**—Alworth 7 pass from Staubach (Clark kick); **MIA**—FG Yepremian 31; **DALL**—D. Thomas 3 run (Clark kick); **DALL**—Ditka 7 pass from Staubach (Clark kick). Att—81,023.

Super Bowl VII at Los Angeles
January 14, 1973

Miami (AFC)	7	7	0	0—14
Washington (NFC)	0	0	0	7— 7

MIA—Twilley 28 pass from Griese (Yepremian kick); MIA—Kiick 1 run (Yepremian kick); WASH—Bass 49 fumble recovery (Knight kick). Att—90,182.

Super Bowl VIII at Houston
January 13, 1974

Minnesota (NFC)	0	0	0	7— 7
Miami (AFC)	14	3	7	0—24

MIA—Csonka 5 run (Yepremian kick); MIA—Kiick 1 run (Yepremian kick); MIA—FG Yepremian 28; MIA—Csonka 2 run (Yepremian kick); MINN—Tarkenton 4 run (Cox kick). Att—71,882.

Super Bowl IX at New Orleans
January 12, 1975

Pittsburgh (AFC)	0	2	7	7—16
Minnesota (NFC).	0	0	0	6— 6

PITT—Safety, White downed Tarkenton in end zone; PITT—Harris 12 run (Gerela kick); MINN—T. Brown recovered blocked punt in end zone (kick failed); PITT—L. Brown 4 pass from Bradshaw (Gerela kick). Att—80,997.

Super Bowl X at Miami
January 18, 1976

Dallas (NFC)	7	3	0	7—17
Pittsburgh (AFC)	7	0	0	14—21

DALL—D. Pearson 29 pass from Staubach (Fritsch kick); PITT—Grossman 7 pass from Bradshaw (Gerela kick); DALL—FG Fritsch 36; PITT—Safety, Harrison blocked punt through end zone; PITT—FG Gerela 36; PITT—FG Gerela 18; PITT—Swann 64 pass from Bradshaw (kick failed); DALL—P. Howard 34 pass from Staubach (Fritsch kick). Att—80,187.

Super Bowl XI at Pasadena

January 9, 1977

Oakland (AFC)	0	16	3	13—32
Minnesota (NFC)	0	0	7	7—14

OAK—FG Mann 24; OAK—Casper 1 pass from Stabler (Mann kick); OAK—Banaszak 1 run (kick failed); OAK—FG Mann 40; MINN—S. White 8 pass from Tarkenton (Cox kick); OAK—Banaszak 2 run (Mann kick); OAK—Brown 75 interception return (kick failed); MINN—Voigt 13 pass from Lee (Cox kick). Att—103,438.

Super Bowl XII at New Orleans

January 15, 1978

Dallas (NFC)	10	3	7	7—27
Denver (AFC)	0	0	10	0—10

DALL—Dorsett 3 run (Herrera kick); DALL—FG Herrera 35; DALL—FG Herrera 43; DEN—FG Turner 47; DALL—Johnson 45 pass from Staubach (Herrera kick); DEN—Lytle 1 run (Turner kick); DALL—Richards 29 pass from Newhouse (Herrera kick). Att—75,583.

Super Bowl XIII at Miami
January 21, 1979

Pittsburgh (AFC)	7	14	0	14—35
Dallas (NFC)	7	7	3	14—31

PITT—Stallworth 28 pass from Bradshaw (Gerela kick); DALL—Hill 39 pass from Staubach (Septien kick); DALL—Hegman 37 fumble recovery return (Septien kick); PITT—Stallworth 75 pass from Bradshaw (Gerela kick); PITT—Bleier 7 pass from Bradshaw (Gerela kick); DALL—FG Septien 27; PITT—Harris 22 run (Gerela kick); PITT—Swann 18 pass from Bradshaw (Gerela kick); DALL—DuPree 7 pass from Staubach (Septien kick); DALL—B. Johnson 4 pass from Staubach (Septien kick). Att—79,484.

Super Bowl XIV at Pasadena
January 20, 1980

Los Angeles (NFC)	7	6	6	0—19
Pittsburgh (AFC)	3	7	7	14—31

PITT—FG Bahr 41; LA—Bryant 1 run (Corral kick); Pitt—Harris 1 run (Bahr kick); LA—FG Corral 31; LA—FG Corral 45; PITT—Swann 47 pass from Bradshaw (Bahr kick); LA—Smith 24 pass from McCutcheon (kick failed); PITT—Stallworth 73 pass from Bradshaw (Bahr kick); PITT—Harris 1 run (Bahr kick). Att—103,985.

Super Bowl XV at New Orleans
January 25, 1981

Oakland (AFC)	14	0	10	3—27
Philadelphia (NFC)	0	3	0	7—10

OAK—Branch 2 pass from Plunkett (Bahr kick); OAK—King 80 pass from Plunkett (Bahr kick); PHIL—FG Franklin 30; OAK—Branch 29 pass from Plunkett (Bahr kick); OAK—FG Bahr 46; PHIL—Krepfle 8 pass from Jaworski (Franklin kick); OAK—FG Bahr 35. Att—76,135.

Super Bowl XVI at Pontiac
January 24, 1982

San Francisco (NFC)	7	13	0	6—26
Cincinnati (AFC)	0	0	7	14—21

SF—Montana 1 run (Wersching kick); SF—Cooper 11 pass from Montana (Wersching kick); SF—FG Wersching 22; SF—FG Wersching 26; CIN—Anderson 5 run (Breech kick); CIN—Ross 4 pass from Anderson (Breech kick); SF—FG Wersching 40; SF—FG Wersching 23; CIN—Ross 3 pass from Anderson. Att—81,270.

About the Author

Pete Alfano is a feature sportswriter on *Newsday* (Long Island, New York). His assignments have taken him to the Super Bowl, the World Series, and many other championship events in a variety of sports. Before joining *Newsday* more than a decade ago, he was a sportswriter for United Press International. He played football at Flushing High School in New York and is a graduate of Long Island University.